# Appealing
# Potatoes

# Appealing Potatoes

Princess Weikersheim

*Illustrated by Martin Williams*

## Hutchinson
London Melbourne Sydney Auckland Johannesburg

Hutchinson & Co. (Publishers) Ltd
An imprint of the Hutchinson Publishing Group
3 Fitzroy Square, London W1P 6JD

Hutchinson Group (Australia) Pty Ltd
30–32 Cremorne Street, Richmond South, Victoria 3121
PO Box 151, Broadway, New South Wales 2007
Hutchinson Group (N Z) Ltd
32–34 View Road, PO Box 40-086, Glenfield, Auckland 10
Hutchinson Group (S A) Pty Ltd
PO Box 337, Bergvlei 2012, South Africa

First published 1981
© Princess Weikersheim 1981

Illustrations © Hutchinson & Co. (Publishers) Ltd 1981

Set in Monotype Baskerville

Printed in Great Britain by The Anchor Press Ltd
and bound by Wm Brendon & Son Ltd,
both of Tiptree, Essex

British Library Cataloguing in Publishing Data

Weikersheim, Princess
  Appealing potatoes.
  1. Cookery (Potatoes)
  I. Title
  641.6'5'21      TX803.P8
ISBN 0 09 143220 0

# Contents

# Preface

This is a new look at an old friend, the potato.

In many ways this unique vegetable has been put at the end of the line, neglected and misunderstood. Few people realize in how many ways it can be prepared and presented as the star turn of a meal.

Throughout my life I have always been interested in food and the right way to compile a menu – learning not to serve three 'creamy' courses in one meal, paying attention to the colour, taking care not to include too many starchy courses, and so on.

But when it came to the point of selecting a potato dish I was in a groove. Roast potatoes, sauté or baked, came to mind. Perhaps a kind of gratin dauphinois or purée?

I knew there were so many other potato dishes, but I had no idea how to prepare them. Probably for this reason I wasn't originally very fond of them – but my husband has always thought a meal imperfect without potatoes, so, purely to oblige him, I set out to find new variations on the potato theme. This meant searching through numerous cookery books, as well as my own collection of recipes, which I have built up for half a century. Gradually the idea was born to put all the potato recipes into one book.

No more racking my brains for ideas, no more blanks. What bliss just to be able to look through that book and have them all at hand. The various everyday recipes, the dinner party and supper recipes, and vegetarian dishes which are a meal in themselves.

I hope my book will succeed in helping those who have the same problem that I had and will open their eyes to the marvellous potential of the potato.

# Introduction

*A short history of the potato*

The potato has a history that is both exotic and ancient, if somewhat hard to pin down. Its ancestor – a member of the Deadly Nightshade family – *Solarum tuberosum* has been traced to South America, high up in the Andes near the Peruvian–Bolivian border, where it appeared as early as 180 A D. There it was the basic food of the Quecho Indians, who knew it as the *papa* and ate it raw or boiled, or sometimes roasted over hot embers. They also used a highly advanced form of freeze-drying to preserve the tubers for winter eating: after the harvest the Quecho left their *papas* out on the high plateaux to catch the night frost. Then, during the day, the families came and trampled them underfoot until all the liquid was pressed out, and the pulp was left in the sun to dry out. The resulting food was known as *chuno*.

When the Spaniards invaded South America in the middle of the sixteenth century they discovered the *papa*. Their hungry army devoured what they thought were 'little truffles'; they also called them 'apples of love', due to their supposed aphrodisiac qualities. When they returned home they brought the tubers with them and introduced them to Spain. Thence, in due course, potatoes spread throughout the whole of Europe. By the end of the seventeenth century, the potato was a major crop in Ireland, and by the eighteenth century it had invaded most of Germany, Austria and France, and crept into the west of England.

Two names stand out in the great debate as to who introduced the potato to the British Isles: Sir Francis

9

Drake and Sir Walter Raleigh. Sir Francis Drake found them in Peru, where it was said he picked them up to feed his crew the fresh vegetables which were supposed to ward off scurvy. Sir Walter Raleigh was supposed to have found them in Virginia and presented them as a special gift to Queen Elizabeth on his return. But, as he never went to Virginia at the time, nor were potatoes grown there, it seems, alas, that this romantic notion must be set aside.

But, whatever the folklore may say, the historical fact is that, by the end of the eighteenth century, the potato had become the most important food crop in Europe. Then, in the nineteenth century, disaster struck. In Ireland, in 1845, a microscopic fungus, *Phytophthora infestans*, sparked off the dreaded disease known as potato blight. Ireland, more than any other country in Europe, relied on the potato harvest. Potatoes and buttermilk were the mainstay, and almost the sole diet, of the Irish people. Meat was rarely eaten as the cost was too great, nor was bread widely eaten. It was both easier and cheaper to grow potatoes instead of wheat on a small plot as a good potato crop would feed a whole family. When the blight struck, the green fields of Ireland turned black overnight. Within a few months the potato supplies gave out and famine set in. By the time it had run its course, this greatest of Irish tragedies had claimed between two and three million lives.

Ironically, it is only since then that the potato has really come into its own, and its true value been realized. France has raised the potato's standing to that of a noble accompaniment to her finest dishes, while in England it ranks as the second most important food crop. The richness, variety and versatility of the potato today is, I hope, best proved by the recipes which follow.

## The potato in art

The potato was a strong influence on early Peruvian art, where you can find those familiar knobbly forms sculpted, first in clay, then covered in gold. The Incas took great delight in caricaturing the various forms of the potato:

monstrous human faces with bulging eyes; animal heads adorned with the tubers. The national museum in Lima has the finest collection, but the British Museum also has a few splendid examples of this early Inca art form.

In Europe, Vincent van Gogh immortalized the potato in his works. One of his greatest paintings, 'The Potato Eaters', painted in 1885, and at least four of his still-lifes, were devoted to it. In addition, he made many studies of the potato as the focal point of interest in the French peasants' day-to-day lives. The women are depicted peeling them, the men are digging them, and they are seen toiling together planting them.

From Ireland comes the beautiful silver or plate potato ring or basket. About three inches high and seven inches in diameter, it is worked with a pierced design of scrolls, flowers and, often, family crests. The ring was filled with potatoes and placed on a white damask napkin in the centre of the table so that the family could help themselves. They are most decorative, and nowadays are rare collectors' pieces.

## Some basic tips

Until a few years ago potatoes were so cheap that there was little point in growing more than a few rows of an early variety. Recent sharp increases in price have, however, stimulated vegetable growers to cultivate maincrop varieties as well.

Potatoes grow best in an open position, so choose a sunny site. They are content in most types of soil, but happiest in well-manured ground. The yield you will get will depend greatly on good manuring and cultivation, but, at a rough estimate, a plot $10 \times 10$ ft ($3 \times 3$ metres) might provide about 100 kg (2 cwt) of maincrop potatoes.

You must take advice before deciding on a particular type of potato for your garden, and how best to plant and grow them, but the following list will give you an idea of the principal varieties of seed potato available, and their characteristics.

11

*First early varieties* (for planting March–April and harvesting early summer):

HOME GUARD: round tubers, good on heavy soil.
PENTLAND JAVELIN: early, white, firm flesh. Good flavour.

*Maincrop varieties* (for planting late April and harvesting in early autumn):

DESIRÉE: a heavy cropper with a fine flavour.
GOLDEN WONDER: an excellent-flavoured potato and a moderate cropper.
KING EDWARD: a heavy cropper with a fine flavour.
PENTLAND CROWN: a large cropper, suited to boiling, baking, mashing or frying.
PENTLAND DELL: produces good crops. Resistant to blight.

Farmers naturally plant the varieties of potato best suited to the soil in which they will be grown and which are of proven appeal to the housewife. While it is sadly not possible to buy a sufficiently wide range of types to fulfil perfectly the requirements of every kind of potato dish, and the virtues of the varieties themselves are affected by cultivation and cooking conditions, experienced potato-eaters agree on the qualities of the best-known kinds. Aside from the inescapable fact that only on the Continent can one find the perfect salad potato and the perfect chipping potato, English needs can be satisfied by the main British strains. For those who wish to match a potato to its purpose, a brief guide appears on page 13.

Buying 'few and fresh' is doubtless the nearest you can get to having your own private supply of potatoes at the bottom of the vegetable patch. This is particularly true of new potatoes – test them for freshness to make sure that the skins rub off easily and that they are damp to the touch. Maincrop varieties that are past their prime are even easier to spot – watch out for any signs of sprouting, green patches or bruising. As soon as the skins of the later varieties are firmly set, you can buy them in larger quantities. Bigger quantities, sold in brown paper sacks,

|  | B | M | JB | R | C/S | S |
|---|---|---|---|---|---|---|
| *Early* | | | | | | |
| Home Guard | **** | | | ** | ** | *** |
| Pentland Javelin | *** | | | ** | ** | *** |
| Maris Peer | **** | | * | *** | *** | *** |
| *Main* | | | | | | |
| Desirée | *** | *** | *** | **** | **** | * |
| King Edward | **** | **** | **** | *** | *** | * |
| Maris Piper | *** | *** | **** | *** | **** | * |
| Pentland Dell | ** | ** | *** | * | **** | * |
| Pentland Hawk | *** | *** | *** | ** | ** | * |

KEY

| B | Boiled | R | Roast with meat |
|---|---|---|---|
| M | Mashed | C/S | Chipped or sauté |
| JB | Jacket baked | S | Salad use |

are significantly cheaper and keep well in the right conditions. It would be ideal if you could keep both a waxy and a floury variety in your larder.

Potatoes bruise easily so handle them carefully. Always store them in a cool, dry, dark place. Warmth makes potatoes sprout, damp causes rot, and light turns them green. Avoid storing them near strong-smelling foods or commodities such as paraffin, which would taint them.

If you peel them at all, peel potatoes thinly; this is not only thrifty, but makes good sense, because many of the nutrients are concentrated immediately beneath the skin. Before boiling, cut into even-sized pieces, to ensure all will be cooked at the same time.

Potatoes are simple, straightforward vegetables to prepare and to cook, but nonetheless there are a few rules worth remembering which will help you get the best out of them.

*Boiling:* Always boil potatoes gently or, as an alternative, try steaming them. Potatoes rarely break up or go mushy if they are simmered gently. The water in which potatoes have been boiled can then be used for making soups.

When boiling potatoes in their skins, wash them and

cut a small piece off one end, to stop them bursting. Put into cold salted water, bring to the boil and simmer until tender. Drain and serve in a napkin, uncovered.

*Roasting:* First, parboil the potatoes in their skins, then peel, and quarter them if they are large. Dust with flour; cover the pan with a $1/16$-inch film of oil and heat in the oven until very hot. Roast the potatoes in it, turning them from time to time, until crisp and golden.

*Baking:* Rub each potato in oil, or with salt if a soft skin is preferred, then wrap in tinfoil and bake. When cooked, cut a cross in the top and squeeze the sides gently to open out the cut, into which you can then insert butter and herbs or other savoury fillings.

*Deep frying:* Use a deep frying pan with a basket. Fill the pan at least two-thirds full with oil. Heat until it is very hot before cooking the potatoes, a few at a time.

To make the most successful chips, slice the potatoes and leave them to soak in salted water with a slice of lemon added, for a few hours or overnight.

*New potatoes:* Whether scraped, peeled or merely scrubbed, always put new potatoes into boiling salted water, then lower the heat and simmer until tender.

*Steaming:* Place peeled potatoes in a steamer above fast-boiling water. Sprinkle with salt, cover with a tight-fitting lid, and steam until tender.

*Discolouration:* If you want or need to wait a while between peeling potatoes and cooking them, simply cover them with cold water to keep the air out. To prevent potatoes from blackening after cooking, just add a squeeze of lemon juice or a few drops of vinegar to the cooking water. This will prevent any reaction with the iron in the potato which causes blackening.

*Peeling:* All potatoes, whether old or new, are best left unpeeled – unless, of course, you are cooking them as part of a soup. Just cut away any blemishes, scrub, then boil or steam as they are. When tender, they can easily be peeled, and the cooking or preparation completed as you require. In this way they best retain their shape and flavour.

*Breaking up:* Most kinds of potato have a certain tendency to break up in the cooking; how much will depend on the individual variety, the growing conditions, and the cooking method used. This tendency will be kept to a minimum if you keep a few points in mind. First, boil the potatoes in their skins; second, place them first in *cold*, salted water and when it comes to the boil reduce the heat and simmer the potatoes until cooked. Fast boiling will not accelerate the cooking, but will certainly increase the likelihood of their breaking up. If, in spite of these precautions, you find your potatoes are disintegrating, pour off most of the water, return the lid to the pan and complete the cooking by this combination of boiling and steaming. But, best of all, steam them entirely.

## A *few nutritional facts*

Despite the fact that in the nineteenth century the potato formed a major part of the staple diet of the Irish at a time when they boasted men of the finest physique in Europe, and today the annual consumption in this country is a staggering 100 kg (220 lb) *per head*, it is still regarded by many as the classic temptation of the weight-conscious. And quite unjustly. The potato is only fattening when cooked in excessive fat or oil. Left to themselves, they carry no more calories than any of the green vegetables (see calorie chart overleaf). Far more to the point, they provide balanced, nutritious meals at low cost, since they are an excellent source of vitamin C, yield vitamin B, and contribute iron and other essential nutrients.

Moreover, the biological value of potato protein is considerable. Potatoes do not cause dental decay to the same extent as other carbohydrate foods, and they may even provide some protection against coronary thrombosis.

On the Continent, faith in the potato's health-giving properties has advanced to the stage where, in Germany at least, it is the basis of a slimming régime. The theory is that if you can restrain yourself to a diet of ten potatoes a day – five at midday and five in the evening – you can lose up to $3\frac{1}{2}$ kg (5 lb) in a week. The potatoes should be served absolutely plain, either baked, boiled or steamed, and always in their jackets. Liquid intake should be restricted to tea or coffee, again taken morning and evening, without milk or sugar.

To treat our King Edwards and their relations in such a miserly, medicinal way would be anathema to most of us, but the nutritional facts behind the diet are doubtless undeniable, and well worth remembering.

**Calories compared 100g portions**

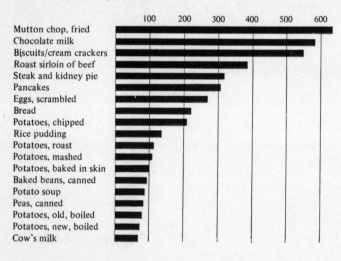

# Glossary of Equipment

BASKETS FOR MAKING POTATO NESTS  These are specialized indeed, but deserve a mention, for they are an integral part of one of the most attractive ways of presenting deep-fried potatoes. As described in greater detail in the preamble to the recipe on page 29, they consist of two metal baskets, of which the slightly smaller one 'nests' inside the other and holds the slivers of potato in shape. When deep-fried, the potato nests make containers for potato soufflés. The baskets are available only from specialist kitchen shops.

CHIP PAN  For deep-frying, either a simple, heavy-based pan or a special, thermostatically controlled deep fryer can be used. Both pans give good results – the obvious difference, apart from the price, being that the former needs careful monitoring to maintain the temperature at exactly the right level. The thermostatic control, the filter system, and the greater safety of the electric deep-frying pans make them a good investment for devotees of the fried potato, although they are more tedious to clean.

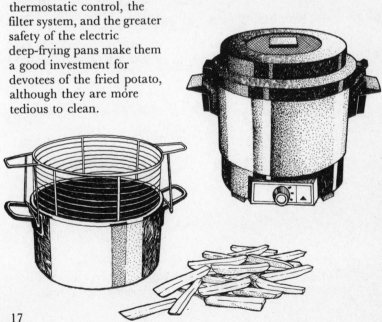

COCOTTE ANNA   Without doubt the handsomest of all items of potato equipment, the *cocotte Anna* is a dish for the potato connoisseur. Designed in France specifically for the famous Pommes Anna (see page 80), it consists of deep, tinned copper pan with heart-shaped handles. The pan can be used as a casserole and its matching, shallow lid – also with handles – as a baking dish; so, although it is expensive, the cocotte is a versatile addition to any *batterie de cuisine*.

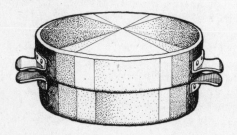

MANDOLINE   A mandoline grater is designed to cut perfectly even slices or strips of vegetable. Its adjustable blade also enables it to cut slices of varying thickness, and it is therefore invaluable in the preparation of potatoes for sautéing, or for wafer-thin deep-fried crisps, or for latticed game chips.

If you decide to buy a mandoline, it is wise to invest in a strong metal one like the model illustrated here. This should last a lifetime, whereas the less expensive wooden versions tend to warp.

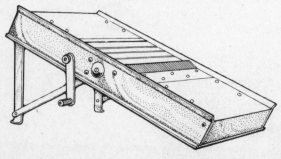

MOULI-LÉGUMES   This French implement may be an old idea, but it still remains the best all-round tool for puréeing vegetables of every kind. Its three different removable discs

will purée potatoes to precise degrees of fineness without turning them gluey — unlike
a food processor or blender.

NON-STICK SAUTÉ PAN   This may seem to have a rather tenuous association with potato cookery, but in fact its perfection over the past few years has provided the answer to those who have hitherto shunned fried food because of its fattiness. Thanks to the non-stick surface, sautéed potatoes can be made with the minimum fat and to the maximum crispness. These pans do need careful handling and cleaning so as not to damage their surface, but they are the most successful available means of sautéing.

POTATO BAKER   This is a simple, usually four-pronged gadget which makes quite a difference to the time taken to bake potatoes through. Its metal prongs conduct heat rapidly to the potatoes' centres.

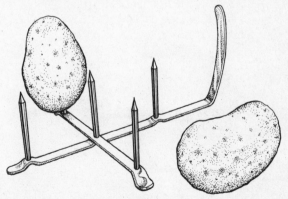

**POTATO BALLER**  A slightly
bigger brother of the tiny
noisette spoon (or melon baller), this scoops out potato spheres,
which are then usually sautéed (see page 40), as a more
sophisticated and decorative variation on the basic theme.

**POTATO CHIPPER**  This is a good investment for habitual
chip makers. If you do buy one, choose a strong, all-metal
model, similar to the one illustrated here. Like the mandoline, it
is worth paying more in the interests of long life
and good service.

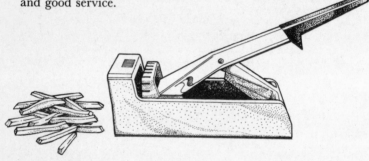

**POTATO DIABLE**  A small, unglazed earthenware pot used
for baking potatoes. See page 31 for a fuller description and
instructions for use.

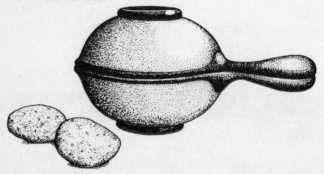

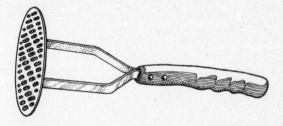

POTATO MASHER This is probably, after the potato peeler, the most familiar tool in the English kitchen. Cheaper and less efficient than a *mouli-légumes* or ricer, none the less – with a good strong elbow to wield it – it works well.

POTATO PEELER Considering that this is one of the first and most obvious items of equipment you will buy, it is surprising how inefficient the most widely available peelers can be. The right ones to look for are those of the kind illustrated here. Made of stainless steel, its beauty lies in the cutting blade which swivels within its adjustable mount, and therefore readily follows the contours of the potato. Some models have a short 'fin' protruding from the blade's mount, which is useful for removing eyes and the odd blemish.

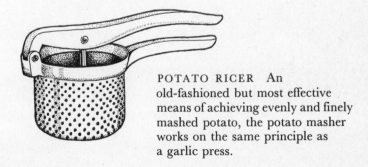

POTATO RICER An old-fashioned but most effective means of achieving evenly and finely mashed potato, the potato masher works on the same principle as a garlic press.

# Basic Cooking Methods and Variations

## Baked Potatoes – basic method

*1 large baking potato per
person*

*melted butter or olive oil
salt*

Scrub the potatoes and remove any blemishes. Push a skewer through the centre of each one (or use the special gadget designed for this purpose – see page 19). Brush each one with melted butter or olive oil and sprinkle with salt and lay them on a baking sheet or wrap them in foil. For potatoes weighing about 225 g (8 oz), bake at 200° C, 400° F, gas mark 6, for a little over an hour, turning from time to time.

To serve at their simplest, and some say their best, cut a deep cross in the top of each potato, press apart, put in a good knob of butter, dust with parsley and season with salt and pepper.


## Potatoes Mexicana   Prince Alfonso Hohenlohe

FOR EACH SERVING

*1 large baking potato
oil and salt
butter
cream*

*yoghurt
paprika
salt and pepper
grated cheese*

Rub each potato with oil and salt, wrap in foil and bake.

Cut off the top lengthwise and scoop out the pulp. Make a purée (see page 32), but this time add butter, cream, a little yoghurt, mild paprika, salt and pepper. Then pile it back into the shell, dust with grated cheese and return to the oven until heated through and golden on top.

These potatoes are perfect with cold meat, but also good with grilled chicken or steak.

## Baked Potato Soufflés

4 SERVINGS

| | |
|---|---|
| *4 large baking potatoes* | *salt and pepper* |
| *50g (2 oz) butter* | *2 egg whites, stiffly beaten* |
| *1 tablespoon double cream* | |

Bake the potatoes, then cut them in half lengthwise, scoop out the pulp and press it through a potato ricer. Mix in the butter and cream, season with salt and pepper and beat to a smooth purée. Fold in the stiffly beaten whites of egg and pile the mixture back into the potato skins. Cook in a moderate oven (350–375° F, 180–190° C, gas mark 4–5) for 20–25 minutes. They should be slightly brown on top.

Serve the potato soufflés at once. They are a fine accompaniment to cold meat or can be served just as they are with a green salad.

If you want to try something special, place a 5-minute boiled egg (peeled) at the bottom of each potato shell, surround and cover it with the purée and bake in the same way.

## Pommes de Terre Aurore

Bake the potatoes in the oven. Scoop them out and put the pulp into a bowl. When cool mix in enough double cream to make a purée the consistency of mayonnaise (that is, not too thick). Hard boil the eggs (one for each potato), roughly chop the whites and then mix into the potato. Dice and fry bacon until crisp and add this also. Season well with salt and cayenne pepper and a little grated nutmeg, then fill the potato shells with this mixture and heat them up in a moderate oven. Finely chop the egg yolks and sprinkle over the potatoes just before serving.

Serve as a light luncheon or supper dish, with a green salad.

## Mimosa Potatoes   Mrs Diana Phipps

Bake large potatoes and scoop out the pulp. Make some scrambled eggs, season them with salt and pepper, fold in some roughly chopped shrimps and fill the potatoes with this mixture.

## Caviar Potatoes

Bake large potatoes (or medium ones, depending on the quantity of caviar available!).

Scoop out the pulp and fill the shell with caviar. Keep lid to cover and serve with sour cream.

## Yorkshire Stuffed Potatoes

Bake large potatoes and scoop out the pulp. Fill with chopped York ham, sautéed mushrooms and a small quantity of chopped onion, fried in butter until soft. Bind the mixture with a little thick béchamel sauce. Season with salt, pepper and a pinch of paprika.

Heat up in a moderate oven before serving.

## Cinderella Eggs

Halve large baked potatoes lengthwise and scoop out the pulp. Put through a ricer, and blend in enough butter to make a smooth purée. Mix in some coarsely chopped shrimps and season with salt and a pinch of cayenne pepper. Fill the potato with this mixture, leaving enough room to place a poached egg on top of each one.

If you wish, you can also lay an anchovy fillet over each.

Sprinkle plenty of grated cheese over the egg. Bake the potatoes in a hot oven (425° F, 220° C, gas mark 7) until the tops are browned.

# Deep-Fried Potatoes

Chips (or french fries) are only one variation on a familiar and much-loved theme – and, if the simplest, by no means the most interesting. By all means learn how to make perfect french fries, but experiment also with the variations given below. You will find them as decorative and versatile as they are delicious. Whatever kind you are making the ground rules are the same: carefully prepared and dried potatoes of a suitable variety; a large heavy pan that will hold a good 3 inches of oil when half filled. Use a thermometer to ensure oil is kept at the temperature required. And remember, do not cover them once they are cooked.

## Chips – basic method

*Baking potatoes*
*oil or fat for deep frying*
*salt*

Peel the potatoes and slice them into sticks about 1¼ cm (½ inch) wide and thick and about 5 cm (2 inches) long. (If you make them often it is probably worth investing in a special cutter to do this.) Put them in cold water with a squeeze of lemon and, if you have time, leave them overnight. Next day take them out and dry them well in a cloth. All starch will have remained in the water. Fry them in a deep frying pan with oil at a temperature of 375° F. Drain on absorbent paper, salt and serve right away.

## Straw Potatoes   *Pommes Pailles*

Repeat the same procedure as in the previous recipe, but instead of slices cut wraith-like slivers. You can achieve this by adjusting the straight and cross-cutting blades of a mandoline. Wrap in a damp tea-towel to prevent them turning brown. When ready to cook, dry them and fry in oil in a deep frying-pan (375–380° F) for about 3 minutes, turning them frequently. Do not fry too many sticks at once as the temperature will fall. When – in about 3 minutes – they are golden, take them out and drain them on crumpled absorbent paper.

Sprinkle the *pommes pailles* with salt and serve right away.

## Gaufrette Potatoes

Peel the potatoes and shape them into neat ovals.

With the serrated blade of a mandoline, set to a $\frac{3}{4}$ cm ($\frac{1}{4}$ in) wide aperture, slice the potato crosswise into rounds, turning it a half circle after each stroke so that you achieve the latticed slices which characterize this variety of deep-fried potato. Wrap the slices in a damp tea-towel to prevent discolouration.

Heat the oil in a deep-frying pan until it reaches a temperature of 375° F. Pat the *gaufrette* slices dry with kitchen paper, a few at a time. Then deep-fry them for 2–3 minutes until they are an even golden colour. Drain on crumpled kitchen paper, salt and serve right away.

## Potato Nests

Prepare and cut the potatoes as for straw potatoes above and heat the oil to 375° F.

Press the potato slivers evenly against the bottom and sides – and right up to the rim – of the larger of a pair of nest-shaped frying baskets. Set the smaller basket inside and fasten the handles together. Plunge the baskets into the hot oil and fry again for about 3 minutes until the potatoes are golden-brown. Remove the inner basket, invert the outer one and slide out the potato nest. Set aside while other nests are being prepared. Serve the nests filled with any of the deep-fried potatoes described in this section.

## Pommes Pont Neuf

Peel and cut the potatoes into rectangles about 7 cm
(2½–3 in) long, dropping them into a bowl of cold water as
they are ready. Using a mandoline, cut the rectangles
lengthways into sticks about 1¾ cm (½ in) thick and wide. If
you do not have a mandoline, use a sharp knife for this
operation.

Heat deep-frying oil to 350° F. Pat the potato sticks dry
and fry for about 5 minutes, a good handful at a time.
Remove and drain on kitchen paper.

Just before serving, reheat the oil to a higher
temperature, 375° F, and cook the sticks for another
couple of minutes, until they are golden. Drain again, and
sprinkle with salt.

## Game Chips

Peel the potatoes and slice wafer thin. (This is done best
and most simply on a mandoline.) Dry thoroughly and
deep fry, once only, for 3 minutes or so, in oil heated to
380° F.

These or *gaufrette* potatoes are the classic accompaniment to roast pheasant.

## Soufflé Potatoes

These are not easy to make, but don't be put off because
with practice and patience you will succeed. The final
results are the lightest of golden ovals of potato, all but
hollow inside. Waxy potatoes are essential to their
success.

The legend goes that Napoleon's chef prepared a meal
for him during one of his battles. The potatoes, having
been fried once, had become cold as Napoleon was late.
When he finally arrived, impatient to eat, the potatoes
were thrown into smoking oil and, to everyone's
amazement, the potatoes puffed out to a delectable
crispness and were a great success.

First, peel the potatoes and trim them to a uniform, oval shape. Then slice them, carefully and very accurately, to 1 cm (⅜ in) thick, using an adjustable mandoline or sharp knife. Wrap the slices in a damp tea-towel to prevent discolouration. The frying is done in three stages:

1 Heat the oil to a temperature of 325° F. Dry the potato slices thoroughly with kitchen paper, and drop them, one by one, into the frying basket. It is very important that the pieces should not stick to one another, otherwise they will not puff up. Lower the basket into the oil and fry the potatoes for 5 minutes or so, until they rise to the surface. Remove with a draining spoon, very few at a time.

2 Raise the temperature of the oil to 375° F, and transfer the potatoes to it, a few at a time. They should puff up almost right away. Finish the potatoes in this way, remove with a draining spoon and set aside. If necessary, they can wait several hours before their final cooking.

3 Just before serving, reheat the oil to 385° F, until it is actually smoking. Plunge in the frying basket for a minute or so until the potatoes puff up again and turn golden.

Remove the soufflé potatoes with a draining spoon, salt and serve.

## Pommes de Terre en Diable

A *diable* (see page 20) is a lidded vessel made of unglazed clay used for baking potatoes, which are cooked without added liquid or fat of any kind.

The beauty of the *diable* lies in its capacity to absorb water from the potatoes, and to give in return a fine, earthy flavour redolent of the best home-grown variety.

The potatoes are simply scrubbed, and left unpeeled, and those of an average size should be perfectly cooked in a little over an hour at a temperature of 350° F, 180° C, gas mark 4.

## Potato Purée – basic method

6–8 SERVINGS

*1 kg (2 lb) baking potatoes*
*150 ml (¼ pt) hot milk or*
  *stock*

*100 g (4 oz) butter*
*salt, white pepper and*
  *a pinch of nutmeg*

There are two ways of making potato purée. The dreaded institutional 'mash' – that stays in one's mouth and makes swallowing difficult – should be avoided at all costs.

Peel the potatoes, cut them into even sizes and put into a pan of slightly salted water. Bring to the boil and boil slowly until tender, then drain. Return to the pan and beat over a moderate heat for a few minutes to evaporate moisture. Put them through a potato ricer or food mill (or whisk with an electric mixer) to make a smooth purée, then return them to the pan. Over the heat, beat in the hot milk and butter. Season with salt, freshly ground white pepper and grated nutmeg.

The best purée is made with potatoes baked in their skins, because the flesh cannot retain excess water and its flavour is perfectly contained. Bake them and then scoop out the contents. Purée and treat in the same way as described above.

## Potato Purée Flambée

6–8 SERVINGS

*1 kg (2 lb) potatoes*
*2 eggs*
*150 ml (¼ pt) double cream*

*salt, freshly ground white*
  *pepper*
*grated nutmeg*
*25 g (1 oz) butter*

Prepare the potatoes as in the previous recipe for mashed potato.

Separate the yolks of the eggs and whisk them into the double cream, then beat these in turn into the potato purée. Check seasoning.

Beat the egg whites until very stiff and fold into the cool purée. Now put this purée into a buttered fireproof dish, scatter small slivers of butter over it and place under a very hot grill for a few minutes until the top is golden brown.

## Potato Nests with Eggs

4 SERVINGS

| | |
|---|---|
| ¾ kg (1½ lb) baking potatoes | grated nutmeg |
| 300 ml (½ pt) milk, heated | salt and pepper |
| lemon juice | 75 g (3 oz) ham, diced |
| 50 g (2 oz) butter | 75 g (3 oz) gruyère, diced |
| 1 tablespoon grated | 4 eggs |
| parmesan | 4 tablespoons cream |

Boil the potatoes in their skins in salted water. Make a stiff purée with hot milk enriched with lemon juice, butter, grated parmesan, nutmeg, salt and pepper. Butter a fireproof dish and, using a piping bag with a fluted nozzle, make a border of the purée all around it and in the centre form 4 small nests. Divide the diced ham and gruyère cheese among the nests. Finally, break an egg into each one. Spread the cream over the whole dish and bake in a hot oven (425° F, 220° C, gas mark 7) or under a low grill until the eggs are poached and the tops of the potatoes golden brown.

## Potato Ring

6 SERVINGS

| | |
|---|---|
| 6 medium potatoes | salt, pepper and a little |
| 3 tablespoons butter | grated nutmeg |
| ¼ cup single cream | ½ cup breadcrumbs |
| | ½ cup grated parmesan |

Boil the potatoes in their skins, then peel them and put through a ricer. Beat in the butter and cream, then season with salt, pepper and grated nutmeg.

Sprinkle a buttered 900 ml (1½ pt) ring mould with the breadcrumbs and parmesan. Add the mashed potato, pressing it down well. Cover with foil and bake in a hot oven (400° F, 200° C, gas mark 6) for 25 minutes.

Turn out onto a warmed serving dish and fill the centre with one or other of the following fillings:

Various vegetables such as green peas, diced peppers, chopped celery or carrots, coated with a ¼ cup of brown butter sauce.

Diced cheese (with, if you wish, a few sultanas added) and curry sauce.

Diced ham, chopped celery and curry sauce.

Hardboiled eggs and tomatoes, sliced and coated with breadcrumbs toasted in butter.

## Duchess Potatoes

6 SERVINGS

| | |
|---|---|
| ¾ *kg (1½ lb) floury potatoes* | *3–4 tablespoons cream* |
| *4 egg yolks* | *salt, pepper and grated* |
| *50 g (2 oz) softened butter* | *nutmeg* |

The key to successful duchess potatoes is to work with dry potato pulp. The easiest way to achieve this is to bake them before preparing the mash. But if you prefer to boil them take care to treat them this way: scrub the potatoes, put them in a pan and cover with cold salted water. Bring to the boil and boil slowly for about 20 minutes or until tender. Drain them, and return them to the pan; beat over a low heat for a few minutes to evaporate excess moisture. Remove from the heat and put through a potato ricer or food mill. Return them to the pan. Beat in the egg yolks and then work in the butter and the cream, whisking strongly. Season with salt, freshly ground white pepper and grated nutmeg.

Duchess potatoes are often used to accompany main dishes. A few possibilities are given below.

## Duchess potato as a decoration for other dishes

Duchess potato, apart from being presented simply in a serving dish, can be used in a variety of other guises: as a decorative border to a meat dish for example, in fluted mounds or individual nests. These can be used wherever mashed potatoes might be, with dishes as diverse as *boeuf bourgignon* and baked eggs.

### Piped borders of duchess potato

> *The warm duchess potato mixture from page 34*  
> *50 g (2 oz) finely grated Swiss cheese*
>
> *a little beaten egg or melted butter*

Beat the potato mixture to make sure it is quite smooth, then spoon into a large pastry bag with a fluted nozzle. Squeeze it out in a decorative design around the edge of a flameproof serving dish. Sprinkle the potatoes with the cheese and either brush with beaten egg or melted butter. Bake in a moderately hot oven (400° F, 200° C, gas mark 6) for 12–15 minutes until lightly browned, or brown slowly, and carefully, under a grill for 5 minutes or so. Serve right away.

### Nests of duchess potato

These are made using the same ingredients and method as described above, but the potato is squeezed out into round or oval shapes. These make a very attractive setting for individual servings of meat or fish, cutlets or hamburgers for example.

### Fluted rosettes of duchess potato

Again, proceed as described in the main recipe, but squeeze the potato mixture out into rosette-shaped mounds before browning and serving, with a spatula, from the platter.

## Potato Croquettes

4–6 SERVINGS

> duchess potato mixture
> from page 34
> beaten egg

> 75 g (3 oz) dry, white
> breadcrumbs
> oil

Make the potato mixture and allow it to cool.

On a floured board form cork-like shapes approximately 6 cm (2½ in) long. Let them chill in the fridge until required, then roll them in beaten egg and breadcrumbs (home-made ones are so much better) and deep or shallow fry in hot oil, until golden brown and crisp.

These are the perfect accompaniment to roast meat and grilled meat and fish dishes.

### Variations on potato croquettes

Using the same basic duchess mixture from page 34 you can proceed with any of the following variations:

### Almond croquettes

Make small balls, roll them in flour, then beaten egg and finally in crushed almonds. Deep or shallow fry in hot oil until crisp and golden.

### Croquette pears

Shape into small pears, roll in flour, beaten egg and breadcrumbs. Place a piece of raw macaroni on top of each pear to imitate the stalk, then deep or shallow fry until crisp.

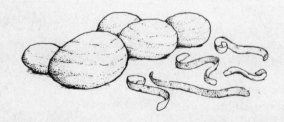

## Countess Potatoes

4–6 SERVINGS

Prepare the duchess potato mixture described on page 34.
Form it into small balls, $2\frac{1}{2}$–$3\frac{1}{2}$ cm (1–$1\frac{1}{2}$ inches) in
diameter. Dip them first in 2 tablespoons of oil mixed with
one white of egg, then roll them in seasoned breadcrumbs.
Lower them gently into deep hot oil (not too many at a
time) and fry until golden brown. Drain on absorbent
paper and serve at once.

## Gratin Dauphinois – basic method

This is just one of several ways of making a *gratin
dauphinois*. The end result is more or less the same and it is
for the cook to choose which way she prefers.

6 SERVINGS

1 kg (2 lb) boiling potatoes        salt, freshly ground
60 g ($2\frac{1}{2}$ oz) butter        white pepper and nutmeg
100 g (4 oz) grated Swiss        300 ml ($\frac{1}{2}$ pt) boiling milk
  cheese

Peel and slice the potatoes thinly. Smear the inside of a
shallow, ovenproof dish with 15 g ($\frac{1}{2}$ oz) of the butter.
Spread a thick layer of potatoes evenly in the dish. Divide
over them half of the butter and cheese, and season with
salt, pepper and nutmeg. Cover with the rest of the
potatoes, butter and cheese and again season with salt and
pepper. Pour over the hot milk and bake in a hot oven
(400° F, 200° C, gas mark 6) for 30 minutes or until the
milk has almost disappeared and the top is brown.

## Gratin Dauphinois à la Crème

5–6 SERVINGS

5 medium potatoes, peeled
  and sliced ⅓ cm (⅛ in) thick
25 g (1 oz) butter
salt, pepper and grated
  nutmeg

150 ml (5 fl oz) double
  cream
50 g (2 oz) grated
  parmesan

Peel and thinly slice the potatoes (a mandoline performs this operation very quickly and efficiently). Smear a fireproof dish with half the butter and arrange the sliced potatoes in it in even layers. Season each one with salt, pepper and grated nutmeg. Pour the cream over them, sprinkle the grated cheese on top, dot with the rest of the butter and bake in a moderate oven (375° F, 190° C, gas mark 5) for about 20–25 minutes. If the surface needs any further browning, put the dish under a hot grill for a few moments.

## Gratin Dauphinois aux Endives

6 SERVINGS

Both potatoes and chicory go excellently with chicken or veal, and here they are very happily married in the one dish.

1 kg (2 lb) boiling potatoes
225 g (½ lb) firm white
  chicory spears
75 g (3 oz) softened butter
1 tablespoon lemon juice

salt and pepper
100 g (4 oz) grated Swiss
  cheese
150 ml (¼ pt) cream

Peel the potatoes and cut into slices ¾ cm (¼ in) thick. Wash the chicory and slice it thickly, crosswise.

Smear a fireproof baking dish with about 25 g (1 oz) of the butter. Arrange layers of potato and chicory in it. Season each layer with lemon juice, salt and pepper, sprinkle with cheese and dot with butter. Pour over the cream, bring the dish to simmering point over moderate heat, then bake in a low oven (300° F, 150° C, gas mark 1) for about an hour, maintaining the heat so that the cream does not boil. The *gratin* is ready when the potatoes are tender and the top lightly browned.

## Jansson's Temptation

6 SERVINGS

This particularly fine *gratin*, more correctly known as *Jansson's fretelse*, is a famous Swedish dish, but who Jansson was or how he came to inspire this delight, no one knows.

| | |
|---|---|
| ¾ *kg (1½ lb) potatoes* | 2 *tins anchovy fillets,* |
| 50 *g (2 oz) butter* | *minced* |
| 2 *large onions, finely* | *salt and pepper* |
| *chopped* | 225 *ml (8 fl oz) whipping* |
| | *cream* |

Peel and finely slice or shred the potatoes, using a mandoline. Butter a fireproof dish and make up the *gratin* in the usual way, alternating the layers of sliced potato with onion, anchovy, salt and pepper and dots of butter. Top the final layer of potato with the last of the butter and pour over some of the oil from the anchovies, and the cream.

Bake the dish at 400° F, 200° C, gas mark 6 for a little over an hour or until the potatoes are tender and the top nicely browned.

## Gratin Savoyard

This is made exactly as the classic *gratin dauphinois*, but the cooking liquid used is beef stock or *bouillon* instead of milk. To some people, this is preferable with red meat to the true *dauphinois*.

## Roast Potatoes 1

Peel as many roasting potatoes as you require, cut them to an equal size, parboil, then drain and dry them. Roll them in flour while still warm.

Preheat the oven to 400° F, 200° C, gas mark 6. Cover the bottom of the roasting tin with a ½-in layer of fat (oil or dripping) and put it in the oven until sizzling. Put in the potatoes and roast them for 40 minutes or so, turning frequently to ensure even crispness.

## Roast Potatoes 2

In this method the potatoes are roasted around the meat they will eventually accompany.

Peel the potatoes and parboil them as instructed above. Rough the surfaces with the tines of a fork, and sprinkle with salt; then arrange around the joint in the roasting tin, about 40 minutes before the end of its cooking time. Baste them and turn them frequently until they are crisp and browned all over.

## Sauté Potatoes – basic method

6 SERVINGS

*1 kg (2 lb) boiling or new*
*potatoes*
*50 g (2 oz) clarified butter*

*or*
*25 g (1 oz) butter and 1*
*tablespoon oil*

Cut peeled boiling potatoes or freshly scrubbed new ones into thin, even slices. Heat the butter or butter and oil in a large, heavy, and, ideally, non-stick frying pan and put in the potatoes. Fry over a moderately high heat until golden, turning them and shaking the pan frequently. Sprinkle them with salt and cover them. Lower the heat and cook for another 10 minutes or so, shaking the pan from time to time. Drain on absorbent paper, check seasoning, and put into a hot serving dish. (Do not cover or they will go soggy.)

If wished, sautéed potatoes can be rolled in softened butter, and sprinkled with chopped parsley or other fresh herbs just before serving.

Rather than being cooked from raw, sliced potatoes may be blanched in boiling, salted water for 2 minutes first.

## Pommes de Terre Parisiennes

These are made exactly as the sautéed potatoes described in the preceding recipe, but first cut the raw potatoes into dice.

## Sautéed Potatoes with Lemon and Garlic

6 SERVINGS

*1 kg (2 lb) even-sized*
*boiling potatoes*
*2 tablespoons each butter*
*and oil*
*grated rind of 1 lemon*
*3 cloves garlic, crushed*

*salt and freshly ground*
*pepper*
*a knob of butter*
*2 tablespoons finely*
*chopped, fresh parsley*
*lemon juice*

Peel the potatoes and slice them $\frac{3}{4}$ cm ($\frac{1}{4}$ in) thick. Blanch in boiling salted water for about 4 minutes or until just tender. Heat the oil and butter in a large frying pan over a fairly high heat and add the potatoes in one layer. Shake the pan frequently so that the potatoes brown evenly and add more potatoes as the first lot colours.

When all the potatoes are golden, toss them with the grated lemon rind, garlic, salt and pepper. Continue to do this, still over the heat, for several minutes until potatoes are well browned and crusted. Just before serving, toss again in the extra butter over a high heat until sizzling, sprinkle with herbs, and lemon juice to taste.

Serve with eggs, pork and grilled chicken or steak.

## Pommes de Terre Lyonnaise

4 SERVINGS

> ½ *kg (1 lb) potatoes*          *oil for frying*
> *100 g (4 oz) onion, sliced*
>   *and sautéed in a little*
>   *oil and butter*

Parboil the potatoes in their skins, then peel and cut them into thin slices. Cut the onions into thin, even slices.

Heat the oil in a pan and fry the onions to an even golden colour. Remove and keep hot between two plates.

Sauté the potatoes according to the instructions on page 40; drain and salt them. Add the onions and mix them in well. Check seasoning, dust with chopped parsley if wished and serve right away.

## Noisette Potatoes

4–6 SERVINGS

> *1 kg (2 lb) boiling or new*          *25 g (1 oz) butter and*
>   *potatoes*                              *1 tablespoon oil*
>                                          *salt*

Peel the potatoes. With a round noisette spoon or potato-baller, scoop out small balls of potato. (You can use the unwanted potato shells later in a soup.) Put them straight into a bowl of cold water, with a squeeze of lemon added to prevent them from discolouring. When ready to cook dry them well in a cloth.

Heat the oil and butter in a heavy frying pan, and fry the potato balls evenly, turning and shaking them over a high heat until they are golden all over. Then sprinkle with salt and shake well again. Cover them with a lid, lower the heat and cook for about 15 minutes more, shaking the pan every so often to prevent the potatoes from sticking. They will be cooked when a skewer pierces them easily.

Drain and salt them. Keep hot but do not cover.

## Truffled Potatoes

4 SERVINGS

| | |
|---|---|
| *5 medium potatoes* | *salt and pepper* |
| *50 g (2 oz) clarified butter* | *finely chopped parsley* |
| *2 or 3 truffles, finely sliced* | |

Peel the potatoes and cut them into thin slices. Dry them well in a cloth. Heat the clarified butter in a frying pan and when the foam has subsided put in the potatoes and fry them gently on both sides until they are two-thirds done. Then add the truffle slices and turn all of them gently until the potatoes are fully cooked. If necessary, add a little more clarified butter during the cooking process.

When cooked, drain the potatoes and truffles on absorbent paper, season with salt and pepper and arrange them on a hot serving dish.

Scatter chopped parsley over just before serving.

# Potato Soups

## Potage D'Arblay

4 SERVINGS

½ kg (1 lb) potatoes (peeled
   and thinly sliced)
1 medium sized onion, thinly
   sliced
40 g (1½ oz) butter

600 ml (1 pt) milk
300 ml (½ pt) water
½ bay leaf
salt and pepper
4 tablespoons cream

GARNISH

1 medium carrot, 1 medium
   onion, 1 stick celery – all
   cut in very thin strips

25 g (1 oz) butter
salt and pepper

Melt the butter in a pan, add the sliced potatoes and onion
and stir. Press buttered paper on the vegetables, cover and
cook very slowly for 5 minutes. Pour on milk and water,
add bay leaf and seasoning and bring to boil. Cover pan
and simmer for 20 minutes. Do not put the lid on the pan
until you are sure the soup is only simmering gently. Purée
until smooth and return to a clean pan. Reheat. Stir in the
garnish (see below), enrichment cream, and serve.

To prepare the garnish, use red part of carrot only, not
the woody core and cut this, with the other vegetables,
into very thin strips. Melt butter in a small pan, add the
vegetables, season lightly and stir. Cover with buttered
paper and a close-fitting lid, and cook gently for 8–10
minutes.

# Prague Potato Soup

4–5 SERVINGS

3 medium potatoes, diced
1 medium onion, diced
1 litre (2 pts) gammon stock
150 ml (¼ pt) approx, of
    thin béchamel sauce, made
    with butter, flour and milk

salt and pepper
marjoram
3–4 tablespoons diced
    gammon
chopped chives
fried bread croûtons

Boil the peeled and diced potato and onion in the gammon stock until tender. In a small pan make the thin béchamel. Season it with salt, pepper and marjoram, add to the stock and boil for a few minutes. Liquidize all the ingredients, then return the soup to a clean pan. Add the diced gammon and check the seasoning. Reheat, sprinkle with chopped chives and serve with fried bread *croûtons*.

# Potato Cream Soup with Cèpes and Marjoram

4 SERVINGS

3 tablespoons butter
1 large onion, thinly sliced
4–5 medium leeks (white
    part only) sliced
¾ litre (1½ pts) chicken stock
2 medium potatoes, peeled
    and thinly sliced

a little oil
225 g (8 oz) cèpes, sliced
salt, pepper and a little
    grated nutmeg
150 ml (¼ pt) single cream
1 tablespoon each chopped
    chervil and marjoram leaves

Melt the butter in a saucepan over a low heat and gently cook the prepared onions and leeks until they are transparent. Add the chicken stock and potatoes and simmer them for about 15 minutes. Meanwhile, heat a little oil in a pan and fry the cèpes gently until golden. Drain thoroughly and set aside.

Put the soup through a liquidizer and return to a clean pan. Add the cèpes and simmer very gently for a further 5 minutes. Check seasoning. Lastly, add the cream, sprinkle with herbs and serve right away.

## Crème Vichyssoise

6 SERVINGS

3 tablespoons butter
225 g (8 oz) sliced white of
   leek
3 medium potatoes, peeled
   and sliced
1 stick celery, sliced
   (optional)

1 litre (2 pts) good chicken
   stock
salt, ground white pepper
   and grated nutmeg
300 ml ($\frac{1}{2}$ pt) single cream
chopped chives for garnish

Melt the butter in a pan and add the finely sliced leeks. Cover and cook gently over a low heat for about 15 minutes until the leeks are soft, pale yellow and have absorbed the butter. But they must not go brown.

Add the sliced potatoes, celery, seasoning and stock and simmer for about 20 minutes or until the vegetables are well cooked. Liquidize the soup until it is very creamy. Check seasoning, possibly adding more freshly ground white pepper. Add the cream, then chill. Serve in chilled soup cups or bowls and scatter a good quantity of chopped chives over each portion.

NOTE: It is not easy to find leeks and chives at the same time as they grow in different seasons. Deep-frozen ones can take the place of fresh chives.

## Viennese Potato Soup

6 SERVINGS

3–4 medium potatoes
4 slices bacon
chopped marjoram, parsley
   and chervil
1 small onion, finely
   chopped
1–2 tablespoons flour
1$\frac{1}{4}$ litres (2$\frac{1}{2}$ pts) veal or
   chicken stock

grated rind of $\frac{1}{2}$ lemon
a few mushrooms, sliced
a few caraway seeds
   (optional)
salt and pepper
150 ml ($\frac{1}{4}$ pt) sour cream

Peel and dice the potatoes. Put them into a bowl of cold water with a squeeze of lemon or a pinch of salt to prevent them from discolouring.

Chop the bacon and fry until crisp. Add the chopped herbs and onion, then dust with flour, stir in the stock, grated lemon rind and sliced mushrooms, optional caraway and diced potato. Season with salt and pepper.

Simmer until the potatoes are tender, then add the sour cream and reheat (but do not allow to come to the boil).

Sprinkle with more chopped parsley and chervil and serve with fried bread *croûtons*.

## Potage Parmentier

4 SERVINGS

3 tablespoons butter
3 medium potatoes, sliced
1 medium onion, sliced

¾ litre (1½ pints) milk
1 bay leaf
salt and pepper
grated nutmeg

LIAISON

2 egg yolks, beaten into 150 ml (¼ pt) single cream

chopped parsley or chervil

This is a finer, lighter variation of Potage Purée Parmentier as the original is much more a purée than a soup.

Melt the butter in a heavy saucepan, add the sliced potatoes and onion and cook them very slowly for 7–10 minutes. Keep them covered but stir occasionally and do not let them brown.

When the vegetables are softened draw the pan aside, add the milk, bay leaf and seasoning. Cover and simmer for about 20 minutes. Liquidize it and then return to a clean pan. Check the seasoning.

Reheat the soup to boiling point, whisking strongly all the time. Then draw from heat, add liaison and reheat gently but do not allow to boil again.

Serve with chopped parsley or chervil scattered over and *croûtons* of fried bread.

Should the soup still be too thick for those who prefer a more liquid soup, thin it down with stock or stock and milk.

## Carrot, Potato and Thyme Soup

6 SERVINGS

½ kg (1 lb) good red carrots
4 medium potatoes
2 shallots or 1 small onion
3 tablespoons butter
1 dessertspoon sugar
salt and pepper

2 sprigs fresh thyme
1–1¼ litres (2–2½ pts) good
  stock or water
grated nutmeg
chopped parsley
4 tablespoons cream

Scrape the carrots and either cut them into dice or grate them. Peel and dice the potatoes, chop the shallots or onion. Melt the butter in a heavy pan over a low heat; put the shallots in first, then, when they have softened but not changed colour, the carrots and the potatoes. Give them a stir and then add the sugar and seasoning. Strip the leaves from the sprigs of thyme and add these also. Cover the pan and simmer over gentle heat for 10 minutes until the vegetables have absorbed the butter. Add the stock or water and cook gently until the vegetables are quite tender. Put them through the liquidizer and return the soup to the pan. Check seasoning, adding a little nutmeg and more sugar if necessary – some carrots need more than others. If the soup is too thick, thin it by adding more water or stock.

Just before serving stir in the parsley and cream.

# Main Course Dishes

# Frankfurters with Hot Potato Salad

Delia Smith, former cookery editor of the London *Evening Standard*, widely followed television cook and author of several eminently popular books, is the source of many inexpensive yet very tasty ideas. This one, from *Frugal Food*, is a typical example.

4 SERVINGS

$\frac{3}{4}$ kg (1$\frac{1}{2}$ lb) potatoes
6 tablespoons oil
1 medium onion, peeled,
    halved and thinly sliced
1 clove garlic, crushed
2 tablespoons cider vinegar

1 teaspoon prepared
    mustard
a few drops tabasco
salt and freshly milled
    black pepper
8 large frankfurters
chopped parsley

To start with, scrub the potatoes well (but don't peel them); then boil them in salted water until they're just tender. Meanwhile, heat 2 tablespoons oil in a separate pan and fry the onion and crushed garlic for 2 or 3 minutes. Then add the remaining oil and the cider vinegar. Stir in the mustard, tabasco, salt and freshly milled pepper, and heat until boiling, then turn the heat low and, at this stage, poach the frankfurters (but check with the supplier for how long, because it does vary). Next drain the boiled potatoes, put them in a warm serving bowl and pour over the hot oil and vinegar mixture. Now sprinkle with the parsley and, using a sharp knife, roughly chop the potatoes. Then serve with the hot cooked frankfurters on top, and have some extra mustard on the table.

NOTE: I always like to leave the skins on the potatoes, but if you like, you can peel them off as soon as the potatoes are drained.

## Stuffed Peppers with Potatoes   Mrs Peter Miller-Mundy

8–10 SERVINGS

10 peppers
6 onions, finely chopped
3 tablespoons oil
1 carrot, finely chopped
5 potatoes, diced small

1 small cup boiled rice
salt and pepper
chopped parsley
¾ kg (1½ lb) ripe tomatoes,
   skinned and chopped small

This is a Yugoslav recipe and very useful as either a winter or summer dish, as it is equally good hot or cold.

Cut the tops off the peppers and scoop out the seeds.

Fry the onions slowly in the oil for 3–4 minutes, then add the chopped carrot and fry both until golden. Stir in the potatoes, rice, salt and pepper and chopped parsley. Mix well. Add half of the tomatoes, stir again and cook over moderate heat for 5 minutes or so.

Pack this mixture into the peppers and wedge them upright into a casserole. Season the rest of the tomatoes lightly and pour them over the stuffed peppers. Cover with foil and bake in a hot oven (400° F, 200° C, gas mark 6). After 20 minutes or so, uncover the dish and bake until the peppers are tender and golden brown on top.

Serve hot or cold.

## Pommes Napoléon   Countess Manetti Bosdari

My cousin reminded me of this dish which we frequently had in our nursery days. It was just a clever way of using up leftovers, but as it was so delicious we didn't mind.

4 SERVINGS

Boil the potatoes (or use up any you may have left over) and slice them. Make a thick béchamel with a little creamed horseradish added. Hard-boil an egg for each person. Prepare the leftovers (meat, fish, poultry, ham or vegetables will all do equally well) by cutting or flaking it into bite-sized pieces. Now take a soufflé dish, butter it lightly and cover the bottom with a thin layer of béchamel. Then arrange successive layers of potato, sliced hard-boiled eggs, leftovers and béchamel. Season with salt and pepper and repeat the layers until the ingredients are used up, finishing with a layer of potato.

Heat in a moderate oven (350° F, 180° C, gas mark 4) then finish by dotting the surface of the potatoes with butter and putting it under a hot grill for a few minutes until it browns.

## Pommes à la Basquaise

Peel large baking potatoes and cut them in half lengthwise. Hollow them out with a scoop and then blanch the shells in rapidly boiling water for 6–7 minutes. (You can use the pulp in another recipe.) Drain and dry them and stuff them with a mixture of chopped tomato, diced sweet peppers, which have previously been sautéed in oil, and diced Bayonne ham flavoured with finely chopped parsley and garlic, salt and pepper (you will need about 50 g (2 oz) of filling for each potato). Butter a fireproof dish, then sprinkle a little oil on the bottom. Arrange the potatoes in it and bake them in a slow oven (300° F, 150° C, gas mark 2) until they are tender (about 35–40 minutes). Sprinkle the top with fried breadcrumbs before serving.

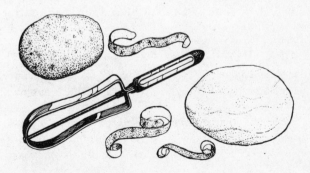

## Pommes Mirette

6 SERVINGS

$\frac{3}{4}$ kg (1$\frac{1}{2}$ lb) potatoes  
50 g (2 oz) butter  
1 or 2 truffles or

225 g ($\frac{1}{2}$ lb) button  
  mushrooms  
50 g (2 oz) grated cheese

Peel and dice the potatoes and cook them slowly in butter until soft but not brown. Cut the truffles into slivers and mix into the potato.

Put all this into a fireproof dish. Pour the Madeira sauce over them, sprinkle with the grated cheese and brown in a hot oven or under the grill.

Instead of truffles, both rare and expensive, button mushrooms can be substituted – cut the same way and sautéed in butter.

MADEIRA SAUCE

300 ml ($\frac{1}{2}$ pt) demi glace  
  sauce  
75 ml ($\frac{1}{8}$ pt) Madeira

1 teaspoon meat glaze or  
  good beef extract

Simmer the *demi glace* and Madeira together until much reduced. Season, add the meat glaze or beef extract and stir until dissolved. Strain.

## Potato Pastry Roulade with Mushroom Filling
Marie Princess Weikersheim

Make the pastry as in the recipe for Potato Pastry 1 (page 83). Roll it out thinly on a well-floured surface and trim to a rectangular shape.

MUSHROOM FILLING

2 medium onions  
oil or butter  
5–7 slices lean bacon,  
  chopped salami or ham

1 kg (2 lb) sliced fresh or  
  tinned button mushrooms  
  (caps only)  
chopped parsley  
salt and pepper  
300 ml ($\frac{1}{2}$ pt) sour cream

Chop the onions finely and sauté them in a little oil or butter in a frying pan. Add the bacon, cut small, and fry together for 5 minutes or so, then lift them out onto absorbent paper. In the same frying pan sauté the mushrooms and when they are ready drain them also on absorbent paper. Put all these in a bowl, mix in plenty of chopped parsley, season with salt and pepper and add enough sour cream to moisten the mixture.

Lay the rolled-out pastry on a large, floured napkin and spread the mushroom filling on fairly thickly (reserving some for the mushroom sauce). With the help of the napkin, roll the pastry up, wrap the napkin round it, tie the ends securely and place it in a pan of boiling salted water. A fish kettle is ideal for this purpose. Boil for 25–30 minutes. Remove from the pan, unwrap and lay the roulade on a hot serving dish and brush it with butter. Serve in ½-inch-thick slices with mushroom sauce.

MUSHROOM SAUCE

Put enough sour cream with the rest of the mushroom mixture to make it quite liquid and serve it with the roulade.

## Salade Niçoise

Despite numerous variations in circulation, the basic elements of the justly famed *Salade niçoise* remain the same – cooked potatoes and french beans. It makes a light and elegant first course or a fine summer luncheon dish.

4–6 SERVINGS

225 g (½ lb) cold potato salad (page 87)
1 small head of lettuce, washed and dried
130 ml (4 fl oz) vinaigrette dressing
225 g (1½ lb) french beans
3 tomatoes, quartered

6–8 anchovy fillets
50 g (2 oz) stoned black olives
1 small tin of tuna fish
2 hard-boiled eggs, quartered
2 tablespoons chopped fresh herbs

Arrange the potatoes in the bottom of a salad bowl. Toss the lettuce leaves in some of the vinaigrette and place them around the sides of the bowl. Toss the beans and tomatoes in a few spoonfuls more and place in the bowl also, interspersed decoratively with the anchovies, olives, flaked tuna and hard-boiled eggs. Sprinkle with the remaining vinaigrette dressing and dust with herbs.

## **Neapolitan Potato Cake**  Marie Louise Princess Windisch-Graetz

6 SERVINGS

*7 medium potatoes*
*nut of butter*
*2 tablespoons grated*
*    parmesan*

*salt, pepper and grated*
*    nutmeg*
*2 egg yolks*
*milk*
*25 g (1 oz) breadcrumbs*

FILLING

*100 g (4 oz) mozzarella*
*    cheese*
*75–100 g (3–4 oz) ham or*
*    salami*

*2 hard-boiled eggs*
*100 g (4 oz) emmental or*
*    gruyère cheese*
*basil*

Boil the potatoes in their skins, then peel and put through a ricer while still warm. Add butter, parmesan, salt, pepper and grated nutmeg, the egg yolks and enough milk to make a smooth purée.

Take a deep cake tin, preferably one with a loose bottom, butter it and dust it with breadcrumbs. Line the bottom and sides fairly thickly with the purée, place over this a layer of mozzarella, then diced ham (or salami), sliced hard-boiled eggs, sliced emmental, and season with salt, pepper and grated nutmeg and a sprinkling of basil.

Cover this with a thin layer of potato purée and repeat until the tin is full, finishing with a layer of potato. Finally, brush with melted butter and dust with breadcrumbs. Bake in a moderate oven (350° F, 180° C, gas mark 4) for about 45 minutes.

## Boxty

Boxty is a traditional Irish potato dish eaten on the eve of All Saints' Day.

*450 g (1 lb) potatoes*  *½ teaspoon baking powder*
*100 g (4 oz) flour, sifted*  *1 large egg*
*1 teaspoon salt*

Peel the potatoes, boil half of them in salted water until tender, then mash them. Grate the remaining potatoes. Next, mix the mashed and raw potato, flour, salt and baking powder into a soft dough with the egg. You can also add a little milk if required. Drop dessertspoonfuls of the mixture onto a hot greased griddle or heavy pan and cook over a moderate heat until golden brown on both sides and cooked through. Serve hot with plenty of butter.

## Bubble and Squeak

Bubble and Squeak, an old English favourite, is an excellent partner for cold meat, and a comforting supper dish on its own.

4 SERVINGS

*450 g (1 lb) cooked potato*  *salt and pepper*
*350 g (¾ lb) cooked and*  *dripping*
*chopped green cabbage or*  *1 medium onion, finely*
*brussels sprouts*  *chopped*

Roughly mash the cooked potato and mix with the chopped greens. Season well with salt and pepper.

Cover the base of a heavy frying pan with a thin layer of dripping and fry the onion in it until soft. Then add the potato and cabbage (or sprouts) and press well down to form a flat cake. Fry over moderate heat until the base is well browned and crisp. Turn at least twice to ensure maximum crustiness, adding more dripping if necessary. When ready to serve, invert onto a hot dish.

## **Potato Gnocchi**   Gnocchi Di Patate

4–6 SERVINGS

> *1 kg (2 lb) large floury*          *1 whole egg, beaten*
> *potatoes*                          *salt and pepper*
> *about 225 g (8 oz) plain*
> *flour*

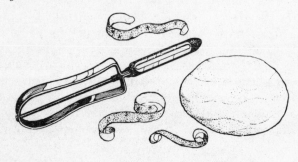

Boil the potatoes in their skins, then peel and press them
through a potato ricer. Place the potato on a floured
surface and knead until it becomes a smooth paste. Then
add the flour, bit by bit, and knead until you have a firm
dough (you may need to use a little more or less flour,
depending on the variety of potato used).

Make a small hole in the centre and put in the beaten
egg and a pinch of salt. Work the egg into the dough and
continue until it is absorbed and the dough smooth. (A
mixer would be most helpful for this operation.) To form
the gnocchi, divide the dough into four pieces and roll
each piece into a cylinder about 1¼ cm (½ in) thick. Cut
each cylinder into 2½ cm (1 in) long pieces. Quickly roll
each piece over the smooth side of a cheese grater. Roll the
gnocchi onto a floured cloth and then into boiling salted
water – about a third of them at a time unless you have a
really big pan. When they rise to the surface, they are
done. Take them out with a perforated spoon and put
them into a warm, shallow dish and serve hot with melted
butter and grated cheese.

Gnocchi can also be served with a tomato sauce and
grated cheese.

## ITALIAN TOMATO SAUCE (for gnocchi and other dishes)

4 SERVINGS

*2 small onions, finely chopped*
*1 tablespoon oil or butter*
*50 g (2 oz) streaky bacon, chopped*
*100 ml (4 fl oz) dry white or red wine*

*½ kg (1 lb) tomatoes, fresh or tinned*
*1 tablespoon tomato paste*
*salt and freshly ground black pepper*
*few chopped basil leaves*

Fry the finely chopped onion in a little oil or butter to soften it. Add the bacon and continue frying until it is cooked. Pour in the wine and simmer until this has almost evaporated. Add the peeled tomatoes and tomato paste. Season with salt, freshly ground black pepper, and basil. Let this simmer gently for 30–40 minutes. Put the sauce through a liquidizer. If too thick, thin it down with water or stock.

## Potatoes with Oregano   Patate Origanate
### Carmelina di S. Angelo d'Alife

This is a south Italian dish, cooked by local people in the oven at the same time as they bake their bread. It is simple yet excellent and Carmelina makes it to perfection, as anything else that comes from her kitchen.

*potatoes, thinly sliced*
*oil*
*tomato purée or tomatoes, fresh and ripe or tinned*
*onions, thinly sliced*
*grated parmesan*

*oregano, fresh chopped or powdered*
*salt and pepper*
*olives, stoned and chopped (optional)*

Prepare the potatoes and keep them in a damp cloth so that they do not discolour.

Into a deep fireproof dish (the size will depend on the number of servings you need) put some oil and some tomato purée (say, a couple of tablespoons for each pound of potatoes) or a layer of chopped tomatoes. Cover this with a layer of thinly sliced potatoes, just overlapping. Place a layer of thinly sliced onions over the potatoes, then a little grated parmesan. Add a good sprinkling of oregano, salt and pepper and drip a little oil evenly all over. If you include olives, this is the moment to add them. Repeat the layers until the dish is nearly full, finishing with a final sprinkling of oregano and oil. Cover with foil and bake in a moderate oven for 1–1½ hours, depending on the quantity of potato used. Remove the foil half way through the baking time, so that the top of the dish can brown nicely.

## Champ

Ireland is the land of the potato and, fittingly, she is the source of some of the best-loved recipes. Boxty (page 61) is one of them, and Champ another. Typically tasty and nourishing, this recipe for it comes from *A Taste of Ireland* by Theodora Fitzgibbon, her foremost food writer.

> *1½ lb (2½ cups) freshly*
> *cooked hot mashed potato*
> *4 tablespoons melted butter*
> *(approximately)*
>
> *salt and pepper*
> *10 spring onions, scallions*
> *or 2 leeks, cooked in*
> *½ cup of milk*

Cook the chopped spring onions, green part as well as white, in the milk, drain, but reserve the milk. Mash the potatoes, season to taste, then add the spring onions. Beat well together and add enough hot milk to make the dish creamy and smooth. Put into a deep warmed dish, make a well in the centre, and pour the hot melted butter into it. The dry potato is dipped into the well of butter when serving.

# Tourte Limousine

This potato dish, a speciality of the Limousin and Bourbonnais districts of France, is a simple yet delicious blending of potatoes with onion, herbs and other flavourings, enriched with cream and encased in the lightest of puff pastry. It is a pie to warm the bleakest winter day.

On its own this potato pie makes a fine luncheon or supper dish, together with a mixed salad. It also accompanies very happily most grilled meat, poultry or fish dishes.

6–8 SERVINGS

*puff pastry made with 225 g (½ lb) flour or 1 large pack frozen puff pastry*
*¾ kg (1½ lb) boiling or new potatoes*
*100 g (4 oz) chopped shallots or spring onions*
*3 cloves garlic, chopped*
*3 tablespoons chopped fresh green herbs*
*50 g (2 oz) melted butter*
*salt, pepper and grated nutmeg*
*225 ml (8 fl oz) double cream*
*1 egg beaten with 1 teaspoon water*

Butter the inside of a 22 cm (9 in) shallow cake or flan tin, ideally one with a removable base, and line it with just over half of the pastry, leaving a 3 cm (1 in or so) border to fall outside the rim.

Mix the shallots, garlic and herbs into the melted butter. Peel or scrub the potatoes and slice them finely on a mandoline and arrange a layer of them in the pastry case. Stir the butter mixture and pour some of it over the potatoes and season with salt, pepper and a scrape of nutmeg. Continue in this way until the potatoes are used up. Pour in half the cream.

Fold the overhanging pastry over the potatoes and dampen it with a little water. Cover with the remaining pastry, pressing it down well over the bottom layer to seal. Trim around the edges and decorate the top of the pie with the trimmings. Glaze with beaten egg.

Bake the pie at 425° F, 210° C, gas mark 7 for about 30

minutes, until pastry is nicely browned. Then turn down the heat to 350° F, 180° C, gas mark 4 (at the same time covering the *tourte* loosely with foil if it is in danger of browning too much). As soon as the potatoes are tender when pierced with a skewer, they are cooked.

Beat the rest of the cream and egg together. Remove the pie from the oven, cut round the pastry lid and lift off; pour the cream over the potatoes, replace the lid and return the dish to the oven for 10 minutes to heat the cream, then unmould and slide onto a hot serving dish.

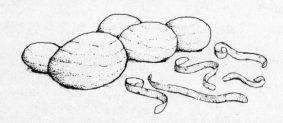

## Potatoes Baked with Courgettes and Tomatoes

4 SERVINGS

| | |
|---|---|
| *5–7 small potatoes* | *oil* |
| *3–5 medium courgettes* | *chopped parsley* |
| *1 large onion, peeled* | *breadcrumbs* |
| *5 medium, firm tomatoes,* | *salt and freshly ground* |
| *peeled* | *pepper* |

Peel the potatoes and slice them thinly (a mandoline will do this excellently). Don't peel the courgettes, just slice them the same thickness as the potatoes. Slice the onion and tomatoes in the same way.

Cover a fireproof dish with a thin layer of oil (not too much) and arrange layers of potatoes interspersed with chopped parsley, breadcrumbs, courgettes and tomatoes. Season each layer with salt and pepper and sprinkle with a little oil. Repeat this until the dish is full. Finish with a layer of potatoes sprinkled with a little more oil.

Bake in a hot oven (400° F, 200° C, gas mark 6) until a nice brown crust has formed.

## Cheese and Potato Fry-up   Countess Rudolf Schönburg

4 SERVINGS

3 large boiling potatoes
2 tablespoons cheddar (or
    any similar cheese)
about 150 ml (¼ pt) milk

2 eggs, beaten
salt and pepper
2 tablespoons butter

Boil the potatoes in their skins until just – but only just – tender, then peel and slice them thinly (on a mandoline if you have one).

In a small saucepan over very low heat mix the grated cheese with the milk until it is dissolved. Off the heat mix in the beaten eggs and season well. The sauce should now be the consistency of double cream. Melt the butter in a frying pan and drop in the potatoes; let them soak for a moment or two to absorb the butter. Pour the cheese mixture over the top, constantly stirring it with a wooden spoon. Turn up the heat to moderate and cook until the potatoes at the bottom become golden; then turn them out, upside down, so that the golden side is on top, onto a warmed serving dish.

## Pommes de Terre au Lard

6 SERVINGS

¾ kg (1½ lb) potatoes
125 g (5 oz) belly pork
40 g (1½ oz) butter
40 g (1½ oz) finely chopped
    onion
25 g (1 oz) flour
300 ml (½ pt) beef stock

100 ml (4 fl oz) white wine
bouquet garni of thyme,
    bay leaf, garlic, clove,
    parsley sprigs
pinch of pepper
chopped parsley

Peel and quarter the potatoes then pare them to a rounded shape. (Use the spare peelings in a soup later.) Cut the belly pork into dice, blanch them in boiling water for 10 minutes or so, then drain and dry.

Heat the butter in a heavy pan and sauté the pork dice. Remove, and sauté the onion in its place, until soft. Sprinkle over the flour and let it colour slowly over a low heat, stirring all the time. This will take about 5 minutes.

Add the stock and white wine and bring to the boil, stirring. Add the *bouquet garni*, pepper, and finally the potatoes. Bring to the boil again, then cover the pan, reduce the heat and cook gently for 35–40 minutes. By this time the potatoes should be easily pierced by a fork.

With a slotted spoon, remove the potatoes and pork dice to a warm serving dish. If necessary, reduce the sauce over high heat to thicken it a little, then pour it over the potatoes and serve, garnished with chopped parsley.

## Potato Soufflé

4 SERVINGS

| | |
|---|---|
| *6 medium potatoes* | *salt, pepper and grated* |
| *75 g (3 oz) butter* | *nutmeg* |
| *150 ml (¼ pt) scalded milk* | *3 eggs, separated* |

Put potatoes in their skins into cold water, then bring to the boil and boil gently until tender. Then peel them and press through a ricer. Beat in the butter and the scalded milk and beat strongly (an electric mixer will do this well) until you have a smooth, creamy purée. Season with salt, pepper and grated nutmeg. Still whisking, add the egg yolks one by one, until they are fully absorbed.

Now, fold in gently the stiffly beaten egg whites. Butter a soufflé dish, put in the potato mixture and bake in a hot oven (425° F, 220° C, gas mark 7) for 20–25 minutes, or until the soufflé has puffed up and is golden brown on top. Serve right away.

## Prague Potato Casserole

6 SERVINGS

| | |
|---|---|
| 6 medium potatoes | 3 eggs, separated |
| ½ cup finely chopped ham | ¼ cup finely chopped parsley |
| ¼ cup finely chopped onions | ½ cup single cream |
| 50 g (2 oz) butter | ¼ cup breadcrumbs |
| salt and pepper | |

Boil the potatoes in their skins, then peel them and put them through a ricer. Mix two-thirds of the potato with the ham. Set aside the remainder.

Sauté the onions in a little of the butter, or in oil, for about 5 minutes, taking care not to brown them, then add them to the potatoes and ham. Season with salt and pepper. Add the egg yolks, lightly beaten, and put the mixture into a well-buttered fireproof dish.

Combine the parsley and cream with the remaining potatoes. Check the seasoning.

Beat the whites of egg, fold them into this mixture and spread it over the top of the potatoes in the dish; dust with the breadcrumbs; dot with the rest of the butter.

Bake the dish in a moderate oven (375° F, 190° C, gas mark 5) for about 30 minutes, or until it is puffed and golden.

Serve with a green salad.

## Farmer's Omelette   Bauern Omelette

The quantities for this popular Austrian dish are a bit difficult to give as it so much depends on the general appetite, but you should reckon 1 egg per person plus 2 more 'for the pot'.

4–5 SERVINGS

| | |
|---|---|
| 2–3 medium potatoes | 50 g (2 oz) butter |
| 75 g (3 oz) bacon, in one piece | 1 heaped tablespoon chopped parsley |
| 6 eggs, beaten and seasoned with salt and pepper | |

Wash and peel the potatoes and parboil them gently in salted water. Drain and put on absorbent paper to dry. Cut rind off the bacon and dice it. Fry until crisp and also put onto absorbent paper.

Using the same pan, cover the bottom with oil, and fry the potatoes to a golden colour, turning them frequently. Place them on fresh absorbent paper to drain.

To make the omelette, melt the butter in an omelette pan and heat gently until foaming. Pour in the whisked and seasoned eggs, pushing them with a wooden spatula as they cook. When the omelette is beginning to set, scatter the bacon over it, still pushing but not stirring. When the omelette is nearly set, spread the potato dice evenly over it. Give it a few more moments, then release the edges and slide onto a warmed dish. Scatter chopped parsley over and serve right away.

## Spanish Omelette

3–4 SERVINGS

| | |
|---|---|
| 2 *medium potatoes* | 1 *large green or red pepper* |
| 1 *medium onion* | 5–6 *eggs* |
| a *little oil or butter* | *tomatoes (optional)* |

Peel, dice and sauté the potatoes (or use leftover boiled potatoes). Slice the onion and fry it until soft in a little oil or butter. Toast the pepper under a hot grill until the skin chars, then peel and slice it. Beat the eggs together in a bowl and then add the other ingredients to them. Season with salt and pepper. Heat up a little oil in a frying pan and pour in the mixture. Fry on both sides until just set.

In Majorca our local cook used to make the omelette first and before it was quite set add the vegetables and seasoning and chopped firm tomatoes as well. She preferred making several small omelettes rather than one large one.

## Carré d'Agneau à la Boulangère

Jane Grigson, one of the finest cookery writers working today, is the author of several cookbooks which are a joy and an inspiration to all who appreciate good food. She has published, among others, *Charcuterie and French Pork Cookery*, *English Food* and the delightful *Good Things*. But it is her *Vegetable Book* that gives us the following recipe for 'Best end of neck in the style of the baker's wife', or, more properly, *Carré d'Agneau à la Boulangère*.

'. . . According to the number of people, buy half a best end of neck of lamb, or a whole one. Ask the butcher to trim the bones and chine them, for easy carving.

Brown the meat lightly in butter, and set it in a large gratin dish on a bed of thinly sliced, blanched potatoes, interlayered with thinly sliced blanched onions and seasoning. Bake in a moderate oven (180–190° C, 350–375° F, gas mark 4–5). The juices from the meat will blend deliciously into the vegetables, and they can be augmented by a few tablespoons of stock made from lamb bones and trimmings.

Some recipes suggest that the onions should be stewed gently in butter, rather than blanched. This can make the dish a little too fatty depending on the lamb, but it does give a good flavour. You can get round the problem by being careful to remove the outer layer of fat from the joint, but do not denude it altogether or the lean meat will be tough.'

# Potato Dishes as Accompaniments

## New Potatoes

Probably the first and finest proof of summer in the English vegetable garden, new potatoes are a delight perhaps best savoured when plainly cooked. At their tiniest and freshest, they cannot be bettered if simply cooked slowly in butter until golden outside and tender within. But, should you wish to make more of them, here are a few more attentive ways of treating them.

### New Potatoes Cooked in Milk

This is a straightforward but delicious way of cooking new potatoes and comes courtesy of Elizabeth David and her book *Spices, Salt and Aromatics in the English Kitchen:*

'This recipe demonstrates a method which turns old potatoes into something special, and makes new ones, as the French say, *extra.*

For each pound of peeled and thickly sliced old potatoes or of small whole ones, allow 1 pint of milk. Pour the cold uncooked milk over the potatoes in a saucepan, add very little salt, *simmer* (if you let them gallop, the milk will boil over and the potatoes will stick, so look out) until the potatoes are just tender but not breaking up. Strain off the milk – it makes good vegetable stock – transfer the potatoes to a shallow fireproof dish, sprinkle them very lightly with grated nutmeg and a little dried thyme or basil, add 3 or 4 tablespoons of the milk, and leave them uncovered in a low or moderate oven for about 15 minutes.

Delicious with a plain roast, with steak, chicken, or just by themselves.'

75

## Kipfler Potatoes   Marie Princess Weikersheim

6 SERVINGS

*1 kg (2 lb) young waxy potatoes*   *butter*
*beef consommé*   *lemon juice*
*chopped parsley*

Kipfler are Austrian waxy potatoes similar to Pink Firs.

Peel and cut the potatoes into ½ cm (¼ inch) thick slices and put in a saucepan. Add enough consommé to cover, bring to the boil and simmer until tender. Drain, then add butter and lemon juice (to taste) and stir in. Scatter chopped parsley over just before serving.

## Glazed New Potatoes

Choose small, even-sized new potatoes, drop them into a pan of boiling salted water, still in their skins, and simmer them until they are just tender.

Melt a little butter in a frying pan and fry a small onion (finely chopped) until it is golden. Add 2–3 tablespoons sugar, salt and pepper and stir well. Sauté the potatoes in this mixture until they are glossy and golden.

Sprinkle with chopped chives before serving.

## Garlic New Potatoes

Parboil small new potatoes in salted water in a covered pan for 5 minutes. Then, sauté the potatoes in melted butter until they are golden and tender, tossing them often to cook them evenly.

Arrange the potatoes with their butter in a hot serving dish. Combine 2 cloves of crushed garlic with finely chopped parsley and coarse salt and sprinkle this over the potatoes.

## Pommes de Terre Cressonière

4 SERVINGS

> 75 g (3 oz) each cream and
>     cottage cheese
> tarragon vinegar
> salt and pepper
>
> lemon juice
> pinch of sugar
> 12–16 small new potatoes
> 1 or 2 bunches of watercress

Mix the cream with the cottage cheese and add, drop by drop, enough tarragon vinegar to make it the consistency of mayonnaise. (You can do this in a blender.) Flavour with salt and pepper, a dash of lemon juice and a pinch of sugar. Set aside until required.

Scrub and then boil the potatoes until just tender. Drain and arrange them on a warm dish. Pour over the prepared sauce and sprinkle with the chopped watercress leaves.

You can serve this dish hot or cold. To serve hot, heat the sauce gently and pour over the still-warm potatoes.

Excellent served with chicken.

## Béchamel Potatoes

6 SERVINGS

> 1 kg (2 lb) potatoes
> 1½ tablespoons butter
> 1½ tablespoons flour
> 300 ml (½ pt) warmed milk
> 150 ml (¼ pt) double cream
>
> salt, pepper and grated
>     nutmeg
> lemon juice to taste
> chopped parsley (optional)

Peel the potatoes and slice them about $\frac{5}{8}$ cm ($\frac{1}{4}$ in) thick. Drop into boiling salted water and boil until just tender. Make a *roux* of the butter and flour, then, off the heat, add the hot milk all at once and whisk until the mixture is smooth. Blend in the cream, season and add lemon juice to taste. Bring sauce to the boil, stirring it as it thickens. Simmer slowly for about 10 minutes, then fold in the potatoes and reheat gently.

Turn out onto a warmed serving dish and scatter parsley over.

This dish goes well with any kind of plain fish dish, with roast or grilled meats, or poultry.

## Dill Cream Potatoes    Prince Alfonso Hohenlohe
4–5 SERVINGS

*2 kg (1½ lb) potatoes*
*a few caraway seeds*
*a knob of butter*
*fresh or dried dill*
*salt and pepper*

*300 ml (½ pt) thin*
*béchamel sauce made*
*with 40 g (1½ oz)*
*butter, 1½ tablespoons*
*flour and 300 ml (½ pt)*
*milk*

Boil the potatoes until just tender in salted water with some caraway seeds added. Cool, peel and slice them, not too thinly. Put into a buttered fireproof dish and arrange them in fairly tight rows.

Make the béchamel and season it with plenty of fresh or dried dill, salt and freshly ground white pepper. Pour this over the potatoes and reheat in a moderate oven (350° F, 180° C, gas mark 4) for about 15 minutes.

These are excellent with fish cakes or plain fish dishes such as grilled cod fillets.

## Paprika Potatoes
4 SERVINGS

*3 slices bacon*
*1 small onion, chopped*
*2 teaspoons mild paprika*
*1 teaspoon salt*

*300 ml (½ pt) sour cream*
*450 g (1 lb) peeled and*
*diced potatoes*
*chopped parsley*

Sauté the slices of bacon until crisp, then crumble them and set aside. Pour off most of the fat in the pan and sauté the chopped onion until golden. Add the paprika and salt and stir in the sour cream and diced potatoes.

Simmer over a low heat for about 15 minutes until the potatoes are tender but not mushy. Sprinkle over them a little more paprika, the bacon and finally some chopped parsley. Serve right away.

## Curried Potatoes

2 SERVINGS

*4 medium potatoes*
*1 tablespoon curry powder*
*1–1½ tablespoons plain*
  *flour*
*1 teaspoon mustard*

*1 teaspoon cayenne pepper*
*salt and a pinch of sugar*
*oil for frying*

Boil the potatoes in their skins, then peel and slice them quite thickly. Mix the flour and flavourings together and toss the potato slices in it. Shake off the surplus before frying them in oil over a moderate heat until crisp and golden brown.

## Potato Cake Galette

4 SERVINGS

*½ kg (1 lb) floury potatoes*
*50 g (2 oz) onions*
*butter or oil*
*1 egg, beaten*

*a little hot milk*
*salt, pepper and grated*
  *nutmeg*

Boil the potatoes in their skins, then peel and pat them dry in a cloth. Put through a potato ricer or *mouli-légumes*.

Finely chop the onions, put them in a pan and soften them in a little oil or butter over a low heat. Then add the mashed potato, beat in the egg and enough hot milk to make a firm purée. Season with salt, pepper and a good pinch of nutmeg.

Butter a rectangular sandwich tin, both bottom and sides. Fill with the potato purée, smooth the top and bake in a moderate oven (350° F, 180 ° C, gas mark 4) for about 1 hour.

Turn out the galette and cut it into slices. It should be brown and crisp and well seasoned.


## Pommes Anna

6 SERVINGS

*1½ kg (3 lb) waxy potatoes
    (more if required)*

*225 g (½ lb) butter
salt and pepper*

Peel the potatoes, trim to an even, oval shape and slice them into ¼ cm (½ in) rounds. Generously butter either a *cocotte Anna*, especially designed for this recipe (see page 18) or a 5 cm (2 in) deep, 20 cm (8 in) diameter cake tin and line the bottom and sides with the potato slices, letting them overlap.

Dot some small knobs of butter onto the bottom layer and season lightly with salt and pepper. Cover these with another layer of potato, again overlapping them, and dot with more butter. Repeat this procedure until the *cocotte* or cake tin is full. The potato slices should be tightly packed. Finish with knobs of butter and salt and pepper.

Using a small plate, press the contents well down. Cover with foil and bake in a hot oven (450° F, 225° C, gas mark 8) for 20 minutes. Uncover, press potatoes well down again and cook for another 20–25 minutes. The *pommes Anna* are ready when golden and crusty, and a skewer pierces them easily.

To remove *pommes Anna* from the pan, loosen carefully all around the sides and under the potatoes with a spatula. Invert a serving dish over the pan, then reverse them, and the crisp brown cake should drop onto the dish.

## Potatoes à la Vichy

Cook the potatoes as in the previous recipe but put a layer of carrots *à la Vichy* between each potato layer.

Carrots *à la Vichy* are made as follows:

*350 g (¾ lb) carrots*　　　　*2 tablespoons chopped*
*15 g (½ oz) butter*　　　　　　*spring onion*
*salt*　　　　　　　　　　　　*finely chopped parsley*

Put whole young carrots, or old ones sliced into strips, into 150 ml (¼ pt) water; add the butter, salt and chopped spring onion and cook over moderate heat until the carrots are tender and the liquid almost evaporated.

Then continue as for the preceding Pommes Anna.

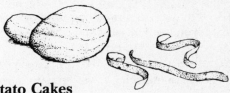

## Irish Potato Cakes

*3–4 medium floury potatoes*　　*about 3 tablespoons flour*
*2 tablespoons melted butter*　　*3 tablespoons bacon fat or*
*1 teaspoon salt*　　　　　　　　*lard*
*½ teaspoon black pepper*

Boil the potatoes in their skins, then peel and mash them. Add the butter while they are still warm. Season well, then mix in enough flour to make a dough firm enough to be rolled out. Turn the mixture onto a floured board and roll it out to 1¼ cm (½ in) thick. Cut into 8 cm (3 in) diameter. Heat the fat in a large frying pan and fry the potato cakes for about 3 minutes on each side, or until they are golden brown. Drain on absorbent paper.

You may serve the potato cakes piled on a dish, but in Ireland, they are traditionally eaten with crispy fried bacon and eggs.

If you roll the dough more thinly, to about ½ cm (¼ in) thickness, they are excellent eaten hot with butter.

## Potato Puffers   Austrian Potato Pancakes

4 SERVINGS

450 g (1 lb) floury potatoes,
   grated
100 g (4 oz) onion, grated
2 tablespoons flour

1–2 eggs, separated
salt and pepper
oil for frying

Peel the potatoes and grate them into a bowl; then dry them well in a cloth. Grate the onions and mix them well in, together with the flour, egg yolks and seasoning: the mixture must be very firm.

Heat a little oil in a frying pan over a medium heat. Take small quantities of the mixture (about 1 heaped tablespoon), flatten and fry them on both sides until they are golden brown. Fry them quickly as they should remain raw inside although become crisp outside.

If wished, you can also beat the white of eggs until stiff and add them to the mixture.

Potato puffers go well with roast meat, steaks or chops, or, in a vegetarian household, served with various salads.

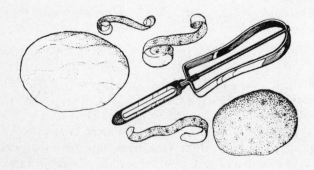

## Potato Pastry

Potato pastry is used a great deal in Austria, Bavaria and many parts of Germany. It appears in both sweet and savoury dishes such as prune or apricot dumplings, sweet and savoury roulades, bacon dumplings and many other recipes.

## Potato Pastry 1

*400 g (14 oz) floury*
*potatoes*
*100 g (4 oz) plain flour*
*25 g (1 oz) semolina*

*1 egg, beaten*
*25 g (1 oz) butter*
*pinch of salt*

Boil the potatoes in their skins in a pan of salted water, then peel and press them through a potato ricer or *mouli-légumes*.

When the potato purée is cool make the dough as follows: mix the flour and semolina into the potatoes, then the beaten egg, flaked butter and a pinch of salt. Work the pastry until it is quite smooth. Let it rest for a while, then work it a little more until it is absolutely smooth. (If you have a mixer, it will accomplish this task quickly.)

## Potato Pastry 2

*500 g (little over 1 lb)*
*floury potatoes*
*about 250 g (9 oz) plain*
*flour*

*50 g (2 oz) semolina*
*1 egg, beaten*
*sugar*

This mixture is used for prune and other fruit dumplings. Make it exactly as described in the previous recipe.

## Sweet Prune Dumplings   Zwetschken Knödel

The German word for dumplings is *Knödel*. These ones can also be eaten as a main course.

Make the dough as in the recipe for Potato Pastry 2. Roll out thinly on a floured surface and cut into small squares.

Remove the stones from the prunes and replace them with a small lump of sugar. Place a prune in the centre of the pastry square. Fold the pastry over to form a ball. Continue until you have as many as you require. Boil them slowly in slightly salted water for about 10 minutes or until they rise to the top. Take out the dumplings, drain them and roll them in fried breadcrumbs and sugar mixed. Serve right away in a hot dish.

## Potato and Celeriac Purée

Celeriac, or celery root, is a turnip-shaped root vegetable, very ordinary indeed in appearance but blessed with a flavour which makes it one of the best of winter vegetables. Allied with potato in this purée, it makes a fine accompaniment to game, particularly venison and goose.

$\frac{1}{2}$ kg (1 lb) peeled potatoes      few tablespoons double
$\frac{1}{2}$ kg (1 lb) celeriac            cream
50 g (2 oz) butter            salt and white pepper

Boil the potatoes in salted water until tender, then mash and set aside. Scrub the celeriac well, peel it, cut into chunks, put in a pan of boiling salted water and cook until quite tender. Drain and purée in a *mouli-légumes*.

Blend the celeriac purée with the mashed potato, beat in the butter and cream and season to taste with salt and freshly ground pepper. Heat through over a low heat before serving. Enough for four.

## Punchnep

Punchnep is a Welsh speciality, a purée of potatoes and turnips excellent with poultry and game.

4  SERVINGS

450 g (1 lb) potatoes, peeled      50 g (2 oz) butter
450 g (1 lb) small turnips,      4–5 tablespoons double
   peeled            cream
salt and freshly ground
   black pepper

Boil the potatoes in a pan of salted water until tender, as also – in a separate pan – the turnips. Drain and mash each one, still separately, then combine them and season well. Heat through over a moderate flame, beating the while to achieve a light purée and to evaporate excess moisture. Finally, beat in the softened butter, and pile into a warm vegetable dish. Make a half dozen or so holes in the purée, fill each with cream and serve right away.

## Potato and Cheese Balls  Mrs Peter Miller-Mundy

4 SERVINGS

*3 large potatoes*
*about 150 ml (¼ pt) milk*
*3 tablespoons grated cheese*
  *(cheddar or similar)*

*3 tablespoons melted butter*
*salt and cayenne pepper*
*1 egg, beaten*
*breadcrumbs*

Boil the potatoes in their skins, then peel and put them through a potato ricer. Add just enough hot milk to make the mixture smooth then, over low heat, stir in the grated cheese and melted butter and beat with an electric whisk until the mixture is very fluffy. Season with salt and cayenne pepper. Leave aside until cool.

Form the mixture into small balls, roll them in beaten egg and then in breadcrumbs. Arrange them on a buttered baking tin and bake in a very hot oven (450° F, 230° C, gas mark 8) for 10–15 minutes, or until they are golden brown. Turn them occasionally so that they colour evenly.

Serve with fried parsley. These potato balls are excellent with fish and grilled meat dishes.

## Potato Schmarrn

4 SERVINGS

*450 g (1 lb) floury potatoes,*
  *steamed or boiled*
*salt*

*1 medium onion, finely*
  *sliced*
*dripping or oil for frying*

This is an Austrian way to prepare potatoes. Take the steamed or boiled potatoes, peel them while still hot and slice them fairly thickly, or crush them with a fork. Add salt to taste.

Slice the onion finely and fry it until light golden in dripping or oil. Add the potatoes and fry them over a low-to-medium heat, turning them fairly frequently with a spatula, until a good, even crust forms. Serve at once.

## 'Turn Over' Schmarrn

This is a good way to use left-over schmarrn.

Take a shallow ovenproof dish, butter it and sprinkle breadcrumbs evenly over it. Put in the schmarrn, press it well down and bake in a moderate oven (350° F, 180° C, gas mark 4) for about half an hour. It should be crisp underneath.

Turn it out onto a hot dish and serve right away.

## Fondant Potatoes

6 SERVINGS

*6–7 medium baking*
  *potatoes*
*5 tablespoons oil*

*75 g (3 oz) butter*
*salt and pepper*
*chopped parsley*

Peel the potatoes, cut them into quarters and pare them with a peeler or very sharp knife so that they are uniformly oval in shape. Reserve the parings and incorporate them in a soup later.

Put them into a pan with cold, salted water and bring them to the boil. Cook for 5 minutes and drain thoroughly.

In a large casserole, heat the oil and butter, then add the potatoes and season well with salt and pepper. Reduce the heat and cover. Cook very slowly for about an hour, shaking the casserole from time to time. Do not let the potatoes brown. Just before serving, sprinkle plenty of chopped parsley on top.

## Potato Dumplings   Fränkische Klösse
### Countess Rudolf Schönburg

Peel and boil some floury potatoes (the exact quantity will depend on the number of servings you require) and put through a potato ricer or sieve while still warm.

Season the potato with salt and grated nutmeg, beat in enough boiling milk to make a mixture the consistency of dough. Roll out to 1¼ cm (½ in) thick and cut into rounds with a pastry cutter. Place in the centre of each a few fried bread *croûtons* and form into a ball. Continue in this way until all the potato is used up. Drop into a pan of boiling, salted water and boil them for about 10 minutes, or until they rise to the top. Drain on a napkin and serve right away.

## Pommes de Terre Hongroise

This recipe is better if made with new potatoes.

4–6 SERVINGS

*a little butter or oil*
*75 g (3 oz) finely chopped onion*
*1 generous tablespoon tomato purée*
*600 ml (1 pt) vegetable stock*

*¾ kg (1½ lb) boiling potatoes, peeled and sliced*
*salt and pepper*
*1 teaspoon sweet paprika*

Heat a little butter or oil in a saucepan and soften the onions, covered, over low heat, for about 5 minutes. Add the tomato purée and stock. Bring this to the boil and simmer for a few minutes. Add the potatoes cut into thickish slices, season and add the sweet paprika (you might need a little more; it should be a good pink colour). Stir gently, cover and cook over a medium heat until the potatoes are tender – for about 15–20 minutes, depending on the variety of potato used.

## Potato Salad

4 SERVINGS

*¾ kg (1½ lb) new or firm-fleshed potatoes*
*olive oil*
*wine vinegar*

*salt and freshly ground black pepper*
*finely chopped parsley or chives*

It is not easy to make a good potato salad without the right variety of raw material to start with. The waxy Dutch kind are ideal, but well nigh impossible to find other than on the Continent. But firm varieties such as King Edward make a good substitute.

Scrub the potatoes and boil them in their skins until they are just (and only just) tender. Drain and peel as soon as possible and dress with olive oil, vinegar, salt, pepper and a good dusting of herbs. It is vital that the potatoes be tossed with their dressing while still warm, otherwise they will not properly absorb its flavours.

## Mayonnaise Potato Salad

Treat the potatoes the same way as in the previous recipe, but omit the vinaigrette dressing. Instead, leave until quite cool, then mix in mayonnaise. Dust with plenty of chopped chives or spring onion tops before serving.

## Austrian Potato Salad

4 SERVINGS

*450 g (1 lb) boiling potatoes*
*2 tablespoons beef stock*
*  or bouillon*
*1 teaspoon wine vinegar*
*finely chopped chives or*
*  spring onion tops*

*olive oil and vinegar*
*  dressing, seasoned*
*  with a little mustard,*
*  salt and black*
*  pepper*

Scrub the potatoes and cook in boiling, salted water until just tender. Drain and, when cool enough to handle, peel and slice them, not too thinly.

In a mixing bowl, pour the stock and vinegar over the warm potato slices and mix in very carefully. Let them rest for a while to allow the potato to absorb the liquids.

When the potatoes are ready to be served, toss again very gently in an oil and vinegar dressing and finely chopped chives or spring onion tops.

## Warm Potato Salad

6 SERVINGS

6 medium, firm potatoes
⅓ cup vinegar
2 yolks of egg, beaten
1 cup sour cream, warmed
½ cup chopped parsley
¼ cup grated onion

2 tablespoons sugar
1 teaspoon mustard
salt and pepper
chopped chives
sliced hard-boiled egg
(optional)

Boil the potatoes in their skins until just tender, then peel and slice not too thinly.

Heat up the vinegar but do not boil. Slowly add the beaten yolks of egg and cook over low heat until the mixture thickens. Remove from heat and cool it slightly. Fold in the warm sour cream and flavourings.

Pour this over the potatoes, mix gently and garnish with chopped chives and slices of hard-boiled egg if used.

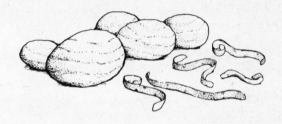

## Andalusian Potato Salad  Marquesa de Belvis

4 SERVINGS

5 medium potatoes, sliced
salt

juice of ½ lemon
6 tablespoons mayonnaise

Simmer the sliced potatoes in salted water with the added lemon juice until just tender.

Thin the mayonnaise with a little of the water the potatoes were boiled in. Warm them gently together in a pan, but do not allow to boil or the mixture will curdle. Check the seasoning and serve lukewarm or cold.

## Potato Salad with Tuna Fish

This is a typically Spanish way to prepare a potato salad.

6 SERVINGS

½ *kg (1 lb) firm potatoes*
*3–4 celery stalks*
*scant 150 ml (¼ pt)*
*    mayonnaise*
*salt, pepper and paprika*
*1 small tin tuna fish*

*25 g (1 oz) melted butter*
*lemon juice*
*4 eggs, hard-boiled*
*4 tomatoes*
*fillets of anchovy for*
*    garnish (optional)*

Prepare the potato as described in the recipe on page 88.

Dice the celery, white part only, and mix into the potatoes. Bind this with a thin mayonnaise. Season with salt, pepper and a pinch of hot paprika. Drain the oil from the tuna fish and mash it up with the melted butter. Add lemon juice to taste.

Place the potato salad in a cone shape on a serving dish and scatter the tuna fish mixture evenly over it. Arrange slices of hard-boiled eggs and tomatoes around it.

Anchovy slices can also be used for garnishing, if wished.

## Swiss Rösti

4–6 SERVINGS

*1 kg (2 lb) boiling potatoes*
*75 g (3 oz) butter*

*salt and freshly ground*
*    black pepper*

Scrub the potatoes (but leave them unpeeled), put them in a pan of salted water and boil until they are almost tender – but they should remain decidedly undercooked. Remove from the pan and leave to cool – if possible overnight – then skin and grate them.

Melt the butter in a large, heavy frying pan. Add the potatoes and sprinkle them well with salt and freshly ground pepper. Fry over moderate heat for about 15 minutes, turning the potatoes over as they brown. For the last few minutes of the cooking time, pack the potatoes down to form a compact cake which is crisp and golden underneath.

When ready to eat, loosen the *rösti* and invert it onto a warm dish. It is particularly good – and typically served – with grills.

*The Gentle Art of Cookery*, written by Mrs Leyel and Miss Hartley, is one of those rare books which retains the quality to beguile and stimulate. It was first published in 1925 and has been reprinted many times since then. These two recipes taken from it should explain a little of its lasting appeal.

## Franklin's Potatoes

'Excellent served with roast chicken.

Two pounds of partly cooked potato; one pint of bread sauce; breadcrumbs, salt and pepper.

Slice the half-cooked waxy potatoes. Make some bread sauce and dilute it with a little more milk.

Put a layer of bread sauce in a soufflé dish and then a layer of potatoes. Sprinkle with salt and pepper, and finish with a good sprinkling of breadcrumbs.

Bake for thirty minutes in a slow oven.'

## Pommes de Terre au Beurre Noir

'Boil the potatoes, then peel them, cut them in pieces and arrange them on a dish, put fried parsley round the potatoes, and pour over them black butter sauce.'

TO MAKE BLACK BUTTER

'Two ounces of butter; parsley; two tablespoons of lemon juice.

Take a handful of small sprigs of parsley freed from their stalks. Put the butter in a frying pan and make it hot. Fry the parsley in it until crisp and brown. When the sauce is brown without being burnt pour it into a very hot sauceboat.

Boil the lemon juice, and just before serving the sauce pour it into the black butter and parsley.'

## Potato Stuffing for Goose

Potatoes make the ideal accompaniment to goose, particularly as a stuffing where their flavours intermingle to their mutual benefit, the potatoes absorbing the flavours of the goose meat and in return countering its fattiness.

For a young goose, about 4½ kg (10 lb) when dressed:

*¾ kg (1½ lb) mashed potato*
*3 medium onions*
*50 g (2 oz) butter*

*1 dessertspoon chopped*
*fresh sage*
*salt and pepper*

Prepare the mashed potato. Chop the onion finely and fry in the butter until soft. Add the potato and sage and season with salt and pepper to taste, mixing well. Stuff the goose with this mixture and roast in the usual way.

## Potato Rolls

*100 g (4 oz) freshly boiled*
*potato*
*about 450 g (1 lb) plain*
*flour*
*1 teaspoon salt*
*50 g (2 oz) butter*

*25 g (1 oz) fresh yeast*
*150 ml (¼ pt) each tepid*
*milk and water*
*1 egg*
*milk, or egg beaten with a*
*little salt, to glaze*

Put the boiled potato through a potato ricer onto a cloth. Keep covered and warm. Warm the flour slightly and sieve it into a large bowl. Add the salt, rub in the butter, a little sugar and the puréed potato.

Mix the yeast with a little sugar and the milk and water. Cream it well and add more liquid if necessary. Cover and leave until bubbles show on the surface. Add this to the potato mixture with the egg. Knead this well to make it into a soft dough (or use a mixer). Cover the dough and let it rise until it has doubled in volume.

Turn the dough out onto a floured surface and shape it into small rolls. Rest them for 15 minutes, then brush over with milk, or egg beaten with a little salt, and bake in a hot oven (475° F, 245° C, gas mark 9) until just golden.

## Savoury Potato Sticks   Miss Langley

These delicious morsels are an ideal accompaniment to
before-dinner drinks.

30 PIECES

| | |
|---|---|
| *75 g (3 oz) freshly cooked potatoes* | *salt and a pinch of paprika* |
| | *1 egg, beaten* |
| *75 g (3 oz) softened butter* | *rock salt* |
| *75 g (3 oz) plain flour* | *caraway seeds (optional)* |

Mash the potato and work the butter and flour into it.
Season with salt and pepper and leave for half an hour in
the fridge to cool.

Roll the pastry out to $1\frac{1}{4}$ cm ($\frac{1}{2}$ in) thick and cut into
sticks about 8 cm (3 in) long and $\frac{3}{4}$ cm ($\frac{1}{4}$ in) wide. Brush
with beaten egg, scatter rock salt and, if wished, caraway
seeds over them.

Butter a baking tray, place the potato sticks carefully on
it and bake in a moderate oven (350° F, 180° C, gas mark
4) for about 10–15 minutes, or until lightly browned.

## Potato and Horseradish Sauce

| | |
|---|---|
| *3 small potatoes, peeled and boiled until tender* | *2 tablespoons horseradish root, grated* |
| *2 hard-boiled egg yolks, plus 1 raw* | *vinegar* |
| | *salt, pepper, sugar* |
| *150 ml ($\frac{1}{4}$ pt) oil* | |

Boil the potatoes, then pass them through a ricer with the
hard-boiled yolks of egg.

· Add the oil to the raw egg yolk, drop by drop at first,
then in a slow stream until it has all been used and the
sauce assumes the consistency of mayonnaise. Add
vinegar to taste, a little water and the fresh horseradish.
Season with salt and pepper and a pinch of sugar and mix
all ingredients together.

This sauce can be served with boiled beef, salt beef, or
baked ham.

# Potato wine

This is one of the most potent of the home-made wines and should be made with care.

On no account should green potatoes be used: they contain lethal poison. Use only old potatoes, preferably ones beginning to wrinkle, and cut away any green parts. White sugar can be used with this recipe, but Demerara sugar gives the wine a better colour.

900 g (2 lb) old potatoes
450 g (1 lb) pearl barley
4½ litres (1 gallon) water
900 g (2 lb) sugar

wine yeast
yeast nutrient
450 g (1 lb) raisins
3 oranges

Scrub the potatoes well, without peeling, chop coarsely and put into a boiling vessel with the pearl barley. Cover with the water, bring to the boil and simmer gently until the potatoes are just tender, but not mushy. Remove any scum that rises to the surface.

Strain the liquid over the sugar and dissolve thoroughly. When the liquid is comfortably warm, add the yeast and nutrient, according to the instructions on the packet, the minced raisins and juice of the oranges.

Cover well and keep in a warm place to ferment for seven days, stirring twice daily.

Strain into a fermenting jar, close off with bung and airlock and leave to ferment, racking when the wine starts to clear.

When fermentation has ceased entirely, and the wine is clear, bottle and store in a cool dark place to mature for at least a year.

From *Drink Your Own Garden*, by Judith Glover (Batsford, London).

# Index

95